TOWARDS A SOCIALLY SUSTAINABLE WORLD ECONOMY

*An analysis of the social pillars
of globalization*

TITLES IN THIS SERIES

Towards a socially sustainable world economy:
An analysis of the social pillars of globalization,
by Raymond Torres (ISBN 92-2-111390-6)

STUDIES ON THE SOCIAL DIMENSIONS OF GLOBALIZATION

Bangladesh, by Rajendra Paratian and Raymond Torres
(ISBN 92-2-111391-4)

Chile, by Gerhard Reinecke and Raymond Torres (ISBN 92-2-111392-2)

Republic of Korea, by Raymond Torres (ISBN 92-2-111395-7)

Mauritius, by Richard Anker, Rajendra Paratian and Raymond Torres
(ISBN 92-2-111393-0)

Poland, by Raymond Torres, Christine Enzler, Gerhard Reinecke and
Ana Teresa Romero (ISBN 92-2-111394-9)

South Africa, by Susan Hayter, Gerhard Reinecke and Raymond Torres
(ISBN 92-2-111396- 5)

Switzerland, by Ana Teresa Romero and Raymond Torres
(ISBN 92-2-111397-3)

STUDIES ON THE SOCIAL DIMENSIONS OF GLOBALIZATION

TOWARDS A SOCIALLY SUSTAINABLE WORLD ECONOMY

An analysis of the social pillars of globalization

Raymond Torres

INTERNATIONAL LABOUR OFFICE • GENEVA

Torres, R.
Towards a socially sustainable world economy: An analysis of the social pillars of globalization
Geneva, International Labour Office, 2001

Labour market, employment, social implication, globalization of the economy, trade liberalization, role of ILO, Bangladesh, Chile, Korea R, Mauritius, Poland, South Africa R, Switzerland.
13.01.2

ISBN 92-2-111390-6

ILO Cataloguing-in-Publication Data

Printed and bound in Great Britain by Biddles Ltd, *www.biddles.co.uk*

PREFACE

The decade of the 1990s began with the end of the cold war and the first stirring of a growing preoccupation with the social impact of the emerging global economy. In the mid-1990s, with the completion of the last round of trade negotiations which gave rise to the creation of the World Trade Organization (WTO), there was hope that a fresh wave of trade liberalization would translate into a substantial improvement of living standards in all countries. The risk that adjustment problems might arise, including in the social and environmental areas, was acknowledged but it was argued that these problems were small and transitory. The World Summit for Social Development in 1995 was a political expression of a more mixed sense of fear and opportunity that globalization was producing. This highlighted the expansion of political and economic freedom, new wealth-creating capacities and growth in social insecurity.

Today the general tone of the debate has sharpened, and public attention has grown ever greater, as witnessed by the WTO Ministerial Meeting held in Seattle at the end of 1999. Concerns are fuelled by the fact that, while some have undoubtedly gained from the globalization process, the economic situation of the majority of the world population has not improved much – indeed, many millions continue to live in absolute poverty. More fundamentally, there is a feeling that many individuals continue to be deprived of basic rights, and that opportunities are therefore unequal. The creation of a level playing-field among and within countries, and questions of fairness, have emerged slowly as a policy issue.

The ILO addressed these controversial issues under the aegis of its Governing Body Working Party on the Social Dimensions of the Liberalization of International Trade, created in 1994. At a fairly early stage, the Working Party came to consider that before speculating on the various types of possible response to the impact of trade liberalization and the globalization of the economy, it would be advisable to gain a better empirical idea of the nature and magnitude of its effects. Hence, the decision to carry out a certain number of "country studies", chosen to offer a balanced sample of situations and levels of development. These studies were conducted with the participation, on a tripartite basis, of the countries concerned. A synthesis study, drawing on the country studies, was also prepared.

A balanced, realistic message emerges from these discussions. On the one hand, in a modern economy characterized by the diffusion of information and communication technology and rapid economic integration, it would be illusory to pursue social objectives under a protectionist trade regime. Open economies are better than closed economies. On the other hand, when implementing open trade and investment policies, governments should not only give higher priority in their economic policies to social issues but should also recognize that strengthening the social pillar contributes to raising the economic returns from globalization. The present synthesis study is a first reflection of these rich discussions. It makes it evident that economic and social efficiency go hand in hand.

A more general lesson emerges from this experience as regards the usefulness of an integrated approach to this issue. All too often, there is a divide between the research communities working on different aspects of globalization. Similarly, compartmentalization exists at the policy-making level and among international organizations. Yet, as in the real life of individuals and their families, economic and social phenomena are inter-related in nature. In an effort to bridge this divide, the ILO Governing Body has decided to renew the mandate of the Working Party as the Working Party on the Social Dimensions of Globalization, and broaden its work programme. This work programme should contribute to developing an integrated framework in three quite concrete ways:

- first, by developing a better understanding of the interplay between social and economic factors in the global economy, not only in general terms but also through a more systematic examination and confrontation of national experiences in relation to specific aspects of social protection and rights at work;
- second, by applying to this search the unique "prism" which the tripartite structure offers for grasping how apparently contrasting economic and social objectives can blend into a single and sustainable process of development;
- third, by associating more closely other international organizations, and especially those which have an economic mandate. The present synthesis study has contributed to demonstrating that this closer association is not only possible but has great potential – without blurring the respective mandates and priorities of each organization – to help all of them, including the ILO, discharge more efficiently their specific responsibilities. The multilateral system is in dire need of a greater capacity for "integrated thinking".

From an ILO perspective, the challenge is to ensure that material progress generated by international economic integration goes in parallel with the balanced development of decent work opportunities both within countries and between them. The Working Party has already made a major contribution to solving this equation by initiating the process which led to the universal recognition of fundamental principles and rights at work as one of the prerequisites for such parallel development. By providing empirical evidence as regards their positive impact on sustainable economic development, it should help create a sense of common ownership of these principles and rights among all the organizations and constituents concerned. More generally, it should contribute to forging the intellectual and institutional tools necessary to make the integrated framework a reality.

Juan Somavia
Director-General

January 2001

CONTENTS

List of figures

List of tables

List of boxes

ACKNOWLEDGEMENTS

In response to a mandate by the International Labour Organization (ILO) Working Party on the Social Dimensions of the Liberalization of International Trade, the Office has completed a series of studies on the social impact of globalization in seven countries (Bangladesh, Chile, the Republic of Korea, Mauritius, Poland, South Africa and Switzerland), and has also undertaken additional research of wider relevance. The Task Force in charge of this project presented the results of this work at various gatherings of the Working Party, and the seven studies were discussed at national tripartite meetings.

The purpose of this study is to provide a synthesis of the main results of this project and to discuss a range of analytical and policy issues of relevance to ILO member States. The study was written by Raymond Torres, head of the ILO Task Force, and has benefited from discussions with members of the Working Party, written comments provided by a number of international organizations and contributions from other Task Force members, notably Richard Anker, Christine Enzler, Giovanni Ferro-Luzzi, Susan Hayter, Rajendra Paratian, Gerhard Reinecke and Ana Teresa Romero. Margareta Simons edited the final version and John Dawson compiled the index.

LIST OF ABBREVIATIONS

EPZ   export processing zone

EU   European Union

FDI   foreign direct investment

GATT   General Agreement on Tariffs and Trade

GDP   gross domestic product

GNP   gross national product

ICT   information and communications technology

ILO   International Labour Office/Organization

LDC   least-developed country

MNE   multinational enterprise

NEDLAC   National Economic Development and Labour Council (South Africa)

NGO   non-governmental organization

OECD   Organisation of Economic Co-operation and Development

SADC   South African Development Community

TFP   total factor productivity

UNCTAD   United Nations Conference on Trade and Development

WTO   World Trade Organization

SUMMARY

Though the term globalization is now widely used, its meaning is not always entirely clear. For the purposes of this report, it is defined as a process of rapid economic integration among countries driven by the liberalization of trade, investment and capital flows, as well as technological change. Compared with previous episodes of economic history, globalization involves enterprises and workers of nearly all the world's countries, in the goods as well as in the services sector. Consequently, the majority of the world's labour force is experiencing the effects of international competition, whereas in the past usually only industrial workers were at the receiving end. International trade and foreign direct investment (FDI) flows have intensified and the information and communications technology (ICT) revolution has facilitated economic transactions. Short-term capital flows have grown spectacularly and, partly reflecting the integration of financial markets, transactions in foreign exchange markets are now nearly 80 times larger than world trade. However, globalization has given rise to a number of concerns: many developed countries fear competition from low-wage economies, and firms from developing countries find it difficult to compete against powerful multinational enterprises (MNEs) from the developed world.

Given the multifaceted nature of the process, identifying a simple relationship between globalization and social progress is impossible. As historical experience and empirical evidence show, the liberalization of trade and FDI has the potential to raise standards of living, but the process is neither instantaneous nor painless: adjustment costs can be considerable. Moreover, the report shows that international trade is associated with greater labour market turnover, with particularly detrimental consequences for workers with only modestly transferable skills. A trend towards wider income inequalities can be observed, not only in most of the countries studied, but also in other ILO member States. There is little evidence that trade is the main direct factor at work here; the adoption of

1

new technology in the context of greater pressures from international competition has tended to increase the demand for skilled labour to the detriment of unskilled workers. In addition, the study documents a near-universal trend towards lower taxation on high incomes, suggesting that the tax system is becoming less redistributive. Between 1986 and 1998, 67 of the 69 countries for which information on tax systems could be collected saw a decline in the maximum tax rate on large incomes; in certain cases this tax cut has been spectacular. Since the taxation of high incomes had reached excessive levels in some of these countries, its reduction may be welcome. However, the phenomenon may also reflect tax competition, since high-income earners tend to be relatively mobile internationally. If the trend continues, governments will soon be deprived of an important mechanism for helping correct rising income inequalities. Since globalization is occurring in a context of increasing inequalities and rising perceptions of job insecurity, many are concerned about the social and political sustainability of the process.

In addition, developing countries are worried that globalization is making their economies more vulnerable to international shocks, especially those that have a narrow export base and whose exposure to changes in the terms of trade is, thus, correspondingly high. The ability of these developing countries to participate effectively in multilateral discussions and conflict-resolution bodies, which often require highly technical expertise, is another area of concern.

Finally, there is growing international concern about the volatility of short-term capital flows. Especially detrimental are the effects of free capital mobility on countries where internal financial institutions are too weak to sustain the large swings in short-term capital movements. The report points to the risk that short-term capital flows, far from being a mere reflection of economic fundamentals, will determine exchange rate fluctuations and, consequently, output and employment levels.

Importantly, none of the countries studied expressed a desire to adopt protectionist solutions. Rather, the policy challenge seems to be to improve the benefits of globalization while minimizing the costs. In contrast to the commonly held view that social institutions and policies would be threatened by globalization, this report advances the proposition that adequate action taken in the four areas of education and training, social safety nets, labour law and industrial relations, and core labour standards – the four "social pillars" – could contribute greatly to making the process of globalization successful and socially sustainable.

INTRODUCTION

Concerns about the effects of international competition on social progress are by no means new (Charnovitz, 1987; Servais, 1989). However, the debate on the subject attracted unprecedented attention during the 1980s, when controversy erupted over proposals to include a social clause in agreements negotiated during the Uruguay Round of multilateral trade negotiations. In the event, no reference was made to a social clause in the Final Act embodying the results of the Uruguay Round signed at Marrakech, Morocco, in April 1994.[1] That same year, the Governing Body of the ILO decided to set up a Working Party to discuss "all relevant aspects of the social dimensions of the liberalization of international trade".[2] At the first regular biennial Ministerial Conference of the World Trade Organization (WTO), which took place in December 1996 in Singapore, the ILO's competence in relation to core international labour standards was explicitly recognized.[3] However, the WTO meeting held in Seattle in the United States in 1999 shows that controversy on trade and labour issues remains strong.

The purpose of this study is to show: (a) that the process of globalization has the potential to raise living standards but that it also entails considerable risks, such as widening income inequalities and increasing labour market insecurity; and (b) that governments have a crucial role to play in exploiting the benefits and reducing the costs associated with globalization.

Part I reviews the international debate on globalization and proposes a simple definition. An attempt is also made to identify the indicators of increasing integration of national economies. The report then examines the possible relationship between different aspects of globalization, such as trade, FDI and financial capital flows, on the one hand, and labour markets and income distribution, on the other (Part II). Drawing on the findings of the seven country studies, Part III examines the roles of social and labour policies, and related legislative and institutional reforms, for enhancing the benefits arising from globalization while reducing the social costs and facilitating the changeover

3

to a more competitive international economy. The report ends with concluding remarks on key research challenges.

Notes

[1] It was decided to set up a Preparatory Committee for the WTO, which would, inter alia, deal with suggestions for including additional items on the agenda of the WTO's work programme. The Chairman of the Trade Negotiations Committee, in concluding comments, also referred to the importance that certain delegations accord to the relationship between trade and internationally recognized labour standards.

[2] Governing Body, minutes of the 260th Session (June 1994).

[3] The full text of the relevant paragraph reads as follows: "We renew our commitment to the observance of internationally recognized core labour standards. The International Labour Organization is the competent body to set and deal with these standards, and we affirm our support for its work in promoting them. We believe that economic growth and development fostered by increased trade and further trade liberalization contribute to the promotion of these standards. We reject the use of labour standards for protectionist purposes, and agree that the comparative advantage of countries, particularly low-wage developing countries, must in no way be put into question. In this regard, we note that the WTO and ILO secretariats will continue their existing collaboration" (*Singapore Ministerial Declaration*, 1996, para. 4). See GB.268/WP/SDL/1/3(Corr.) and Add.1, and http://www.wto.org/wto/archives/mc.htm.

PART I

GLOBALIZATION: PERCEPTIONS, DEFINITION AND MEASUREMENT

A. THE INTERNATIONAL DEBATE

Today, globalization is one of the most widely used terms in debates on economic and social development. However, opinions on the effects of globalization could not be more divergent: while some see it as a driving force towards new prosperity in which poorer countries have the chance to catch up with the world economy, others fear that it will have adverse effects on workers, jeopardize their social rights and increase social inequalities.

Although it is generally perceived as inevitable, globalization has raised fears in developed and developing countries alike. Developed countries are mainly concerned about the competition of cheaper imported goods from developing countries, while the latter economies fear that they will be unable to compete with developed countries in a liberalized environment and will thus become marginalized. Furthermore, developing countries generally believe that globalization requires economic reforms that will cause considerable short- and long-term hardship.

Part of the uneasiness about globalization stems from the perception that national policies are increasingly being dictated by international constraints; macroeconomic imbalances can certainly be more difficult to sustain economically in a liberalized environment than in one that is relatively more protected. Indeed, in some cases globalization is being used to justify certain policy measures, such as, for example, cutbacks in social protection schemes.[1]

Before examining whether these concerns are justified or not, it is important to define the terms and concepts used in this report. And, although globalization has economic, political and cultural dimensions, all of which can have a significant impact on the social environment, this report focuses on the economic effects of globalization.

B. A SIMPLE DEFINITION

Economic globalization can be simply defined as a process of rapid economic integration between countries. It therefore embraces the increased integration of product and factor markets, as well as the speed with which this integration takes place. Globalization has been driven by the liberalization of international trade and FDI, and by freer capital flows, and manifests itself mainly through an intensification of activities in the following areas:

- international trade in goods and services;
- capital flows (FDI and short-term flows);
- the role of MNEs;
- the reorganization of production networks on an international scale;
- the adoption of new technology, notably ICT.

The different dimensions of the process are interrelated and mutually reinforcing. Thus, information flows that enable real-time transactions not only facilitate international trade and investment but also make it possible for enterprises to stay informed of international prices for the inputs they require so that they can obtain similar price levels from their national providers. So, although no trade may actually take place, this will still have an impact on local enterprises. The international flow of "soft" technology – the knowledge of management practices and the methods of work organization – is another facet of globalization. Importantly, international migration policies remain relatively protective (except within certain free-trade areas) and, as a result, the trend towards a rise in the number of cross-border movements of workers is much less pronounced than that of capital and goods.

C. MEASURING GLOBALIZATION

Some observers argue that today's economy is no more globalized than it was in earlier periods of capitalism. However, the measures of globalization available today, imperfect though they may be, show that, on the contrary, the world economy has never been so integrated.

Trade flows

The increase in trade flows can be illustrated by looking at the trends in the share of exports of goods and services in gross domestic product (GDP). Some authors have compared contemporary trade flows with historical data, and have come to the conclusion that the trade/GDP ratio increased at a rapid pace during the nineteenth and early twentieth centuries. A similar trend can be discerned between 1950 and the early 1970s. So, it is argued, the world has been observing periods of increasing and diminishing openness in trade for some time now. Some commentators have even claimed that the world is less economically open today than it was at the beginning of the twentieth century.

Although this historical perspective is enlightening, it would be an exaggeration to claim that today's economy is no more globalized than it was early in the twentieth century. As table 1 shows, for most countries for which long-term data are available, the share of exports in GDP is higher now than ever before in modern history.

Figure 1A shows that world exports as a share of world GDP in current prices recorded rapid growth from the mid-1960s to the mid-1970s, and, following a period of stagnation between the mid-1970s and the mid-1980s, have since resumed a steep upward trend. Today, world exports account for nearly one-fifth of world GDP, that is, 5 percentage points more than in the mid-1980s. At constant prices, the increase is much more pronounced, reflecting the fact that, on average, export prices have grown at a slower pace than the

Table 1   Merchandise exports as a percentage of GDP in selected countries, 1820–1996[1]   (exports and GDP [purchasing power parity] at constant prices)

Country/area	1820	1870	1913	1929	1950	1973	1992	1996[2]
France	1.3	4.9	8.2	8.6	7.7	15.4	22.9	26.0
Germany	n.a.	9.5	15.6	12.8	6.2	23.8	32.6	n.a.
Netherlands	n.a.	17.5	17.8	17.2	12.5	41.7	55.3	60.4
United Kingdom	3.1	12.0	17.7	13.3	11.4	14.0	21.4	25.4
Total Western Europe[3]	**n.a.**	**10.0**	**16.3**	**13.3**	**9.4**	**20.9**	**29.7**	**34.6**
Spain	1.1	3.8	8.1	5.0	1.6	5.0	13.4	20.3
USSR/Russian Federation	n.a.	n.a.	2.9	1.6	1.3	3.8	5.1	n.a.
Australia	n.a.	7.4	12.8	11.2	9.1	11.2	16.9	18.1
Canada	n.a.	12.0	12.2	15.8	13.0	19.9	27.2	37.2
United States	2.0	2.5	3.7	3.6	3.0	5.0	8.2	10.0
Argentina	n.a.	9.4	6.8	6.1	2.4	2.1	4.3	6.8
Brazil	n.a.	11.8	9.5	7.1	4.0	2.6	4.7	4.9
Mexico	n.a.	3.7	10.8	14.8	3.5	2.2	6.4	9.0
Total Latin America[4]	**n.a.**	**9.0**	**9.5**	**9.7**	**6.2**	**4.6**	**6.2**	**8.1**
China	n.a.	0.7	1.4	1.7	1.9	1.1	2.3	2.4
India	n.a.	2.5	4.7	3.7	2.6	2.0	1.7	2.2
Indonesia	n.a.	0.9	2.2	3.6	3.3	5.0	7.4	7.1
Japan	n.a.	0.2	2.4	3.5	2.3	7.9	12.4	13.2
Korea, Republic of	0.0	0.0	1.0	4.5	1.0	8.2	17.8	23.8
Thailand	n.a.	2.1	6.7	6.6	7.0	4.5	11.4	12.5
Taiwan, China	–	–	2.5	5.2	2.5	10.2	34.4	n.a.
Total Asia[5]	**n.a.**	**1.3**	**2.6**	**2.8**	**2.3**	**4.4**	**7.2**	**7.4**
World	**1.0**	**5.0**	**8.7**	**9.0**	**7.0**	**11.2**	**13.5**	**16.0**

n.a. = data not available; – = not applicable.

[1] Data from 1820 to 1992 come from Maddison (1995) and are calculated as the ratio of exports in US dollars and GDP at PPP in 1990 constant prices. Data for 1996 are ILO Task Force estimates, based on World Bank (1998) data. The series was obtained after adjustment for consistency with the Maddison series. [2] Data for the Netherlands, Australia, Brazil, China, Indonesia, Total Western Europe, Total Latin America, Total Asia and World refer to 1995, not 1996. [3] Total Western Europe includes Austria, Belgium, Denmark, Finland, France, Germany, Italy, Netherlands, Norway, Sweden, Switzerland and the United Kingdom; 1995 data for Total Western Europe do not include Germany. [4] Total Latin America includes Argentina, Brazil, Chile, Colombia, Mexico, Peru and Venezuela. [5] Total Asia includes Bangladesh, China, India, Indonesia, Japan, Myanmar, Pakistan, Philippines, Republic of Korea, Taiwan (China) and Thailand; 1995 data for Total Asia do not include Taiwan (China) and Myanmar.

Sources: A. Maddison (1995) and ILO Task Force, based on World Bank data (1998).

Figure 1   World exports of goods and services as a share of world gross
domestic product (GDP), 1960–98

A. Current prices

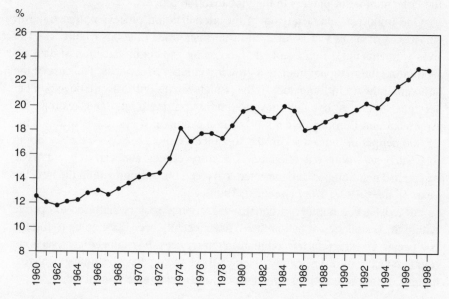

B. Constant prices

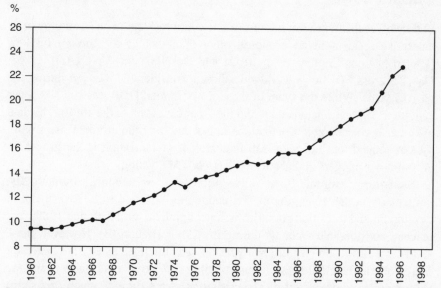

Sources: ILO Task Force, based on data from IMF: *World Economic Outlook* (May 1999); and World Bank: *World Development Indicators* (1999).

prices for domestically produced goods and services (figure 1B). The recent rise in the exports/GDP ratio has been much stronger in low- and middle-income countries than in high-income countries (figure 2). This trend reflects the large number of players in the globalization process.

One important characteristic of the globalization process is that trade in services is rising as fast as, or even faster than, trade in goods (figure 3).[2] The improvements made in the storage, processing and communication of data are facilitating international trade in a growing number of services. The case of the software industry in Bangalore, India, which carries out software development services, such as detailed design, coding/programming and testing, for American and European clients is but one example. It is estimated that some 25,000 people in India work in the so-called "remote services", that is, doing jobs such as typing out telephone directory entries and carrying out basic research. Their numbers are expected to exceed one million within the next ten years (Lateef, 1997; *The Economist*, 1999).

Moreover, in a number of countries, economic sectors that used to operate within the boundaries of nation States have recently been opening up to foreign companies; construction, telecommunication services and engineering projects are important examples. The extent to which these sectors have become globalized, though, cannot be easily discerned, since little actual trade is involved.

Capital flows

FDI involves the long-term interest of one entity resident in one economy in an enterprise resident in an economy other than that of the foreign investor (United Nations Conference on Trade and Development [UNCTAD], 1998). Data on gross FDI flows worldwide show a considerable increase during the past 15 years. While the share of these flows in total GDP was below 1.5 per cent up to 1986, it fluctuated around the 2 per cent level in the 1990s. The data also reveal considerable fluctuations rather than an uninterrupted rise (figure 4A). A related, but not identical, indicator of globalization is the growth in cross-border mergers and acquisitions (UNCTAD, various years).

Short-term capital flows have increased even more dramatically, particularly in the "emerging market economies". Net portfolio investment in developing and transition countries was negligible in the 1970s and 1980s, but reached considerable amounts during the 1990s (figure 4B). However, these short-term flows show significant year-on-year fluctuations and are generally more volatile than FDI flows.[3] This volatility can create an unstable economic environment, as witnessed by the crisis that swept through much of Asia in 1997–98 (see Part II for a discussion of this issue).

Figure 2 Exports of goods and services as a share of GDP by group of countries, 1987–97 (at current prices)

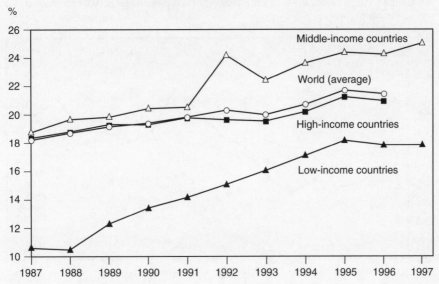

Source: World Bank: *World Development Indicators* (1999).

Figure 3 World exports of services as a share of total world exports, 1975–98

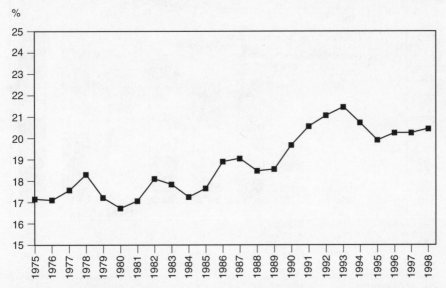

Sources: ILO Task Force, based on data from IMF: *World Economic Outlook* (May 1999); and World Bank: *World Development Indicators* (1999).

13

Figure 4   Trends in capital flows

A. Gross foreign direct investment, 1980–97 (as a percentage of GDP, purchasing power parity [PPP])

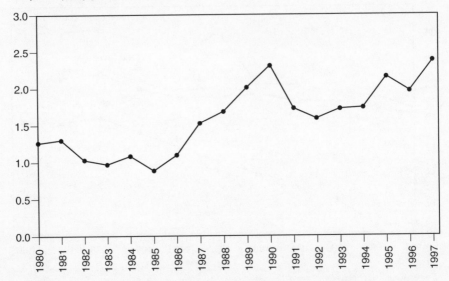

B. Net capital flows to developing and transition countries, 1970–96 (in billions of US dollars)

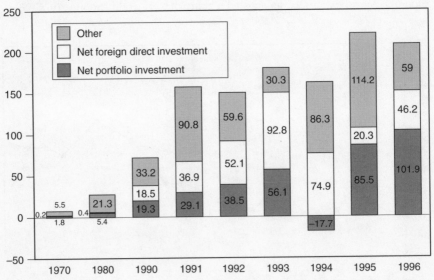

Note: Other capital flows include short- and long-term trade credits, loans, currency and deposits, and other accounts receivable and payable.

Sources: ILO Task Force, based on data from the World Bank: *World Development Indicators* (1999); and Knight (1998).

Table 2   Comparison of world exports and turnover in foreign exchange
markets, 1989–98[1] (in billions of US dollars)

	1989	1992	1995	1998
Ratio of net turnover in foreign exchange markets to exports	55.6	63.5	69.7	78.0
Average daily net turnover in foreign exchange markets	590	820	1 190	1 490
Exports of goods and services, daily average	10.6	12.9	17.1	19.1[2]

[1] Figures for net turnover in foreign exchange markets refer to a number of reporting sample countries. Turnover data and turnover/export ratios are thus underestimations. [2] Export data for 1998 are preliminary.

Sources: ILO Task Force based on data from the Bank for International Settlements (1998); World Bank (1998); and IMF (1998).

The importance that short-term financial transactions have acquired in the international economy is illustrated by the fact that their value is much higher than the volume of the exchange of goods and services. The worldwide daily turnover in foreign exchange markets in 1998 was at least 78 times the daily volume of the exports of goods and services, up from 56 times in 1989 (table 2).

Multinational enterprises and the reorganization of production networks

Enterprises are increasingly working on an international scale. The enhanced ICT and transport facilities (and the consequent declining costs of moving information or goods from one country to another) help make the globalization process more encompassing than previous episodes of international integration. The increasing role of MNEs in the international economy can be measured by the share of the production of foreign affiliates in world GDP. This share increased from around 5 per cent in the early 1980s to almost 7 per cent in 1996–97 (UNCTAD, 1998).

In order to adapt to increasing international competition, enterprises are not only introducing more flexibility into their internal operations, but they are also changing their relationships with domestic and foreign enterprises. Many enterprises are now concentrating on core activities (i.e. activities that are unique or difficult to imitate and are of high value) and those activities that can provide a gateway to new markets (Palpacuer, 1998). Focusing on core areas of competence allows firms not only to develop superior capabilities through specializing but also to find new ways of taking advantage of their environment. By externalizing non-core activities, firms can reduce their fixed costs and thus enhance their ability to shift resources quickly and seize new opportunities in response to unexpected changes in supply and demand.

The outsourcing of inputs or services can occur on a national and international basis. For example, recent developments indicate that large auto-manufacturers are now implementing these network strategies on a global scale, relying on selected subcontractors to supply particular components for their worldwide operations (Humphrey, 1998). European and American garment enterprises have been progressively extending their subcontracting networks to Asia and Latin America, and even garment producers in middle-income countries such as Chile are increasingly outsourcing labour-intensive parts of the production process to developing countries in Asia (Reinecke and Torres, 2001).

For the manufacturing sector as a whole, the extent of international outsourcing can be measured by the increased share of imported inputs in total inputs, as documented for countries such as Canada, Mexico, the United Kingdom and the United States.[4]

Notes

[1] There is, however, no empirical backing for the argument that countries with relatively "open" economies have less-developed social protection systems than those with more "closed" economies. If anything, it appears that countries exposed to higher levels of external risk have higher levels of government spending on welfare than countries that are less exposed (Rodrik, 1997). Thus, while the reform of social protection systems to make them more effective and efficient may be necessary with or without globalization, the dismantling of social protection systems cannot be justified on the grounds of external constraints. It is nevertheless true that, as capital becomes increasingly mobile, the tax base is being partly eroded, making it more difficult to finance social benefits.

[2] This trend should be treated with caution, since the rise in services may be partly attributable to the improved coverage of trade statistics in that field.

[3] In its 1998 *World Investment Report* (pp. 14–16), UNCTAD presented calculations for the 1992–97 period that confirmed the higher volatility coefficients for portfolio investment compared with FDI. Commercial bank loans proved an even more volatile source of capital.

[4] See Feenstra and Hanson (1995); Hanson and Harrison (1995). By contrast, the use of imported inputs decreased in Japan between the 1970s and the 1990s. It is also interesting to note that certain firms that outsourced part of their activities have reportedly admitted that the economic outcome of their decisions has not met their expectations. A process of re-internalization may hence take place in certain cases.

PART II

THE SOCIAL IMPACT OF GLOBALIZATION

A. INTRODUCTION

It is extremely difficult to assess the consequences of a complex and all-embracing phenomenon such as globalization, since there are substantial theoretical, methodological and empirical problems involved. It is particularly difficult to isolate empirically the impact of any single dimension of globalization from the impact of other economic or political changes. Also, for the moment it is only possible to quantify its short-term effects, while long-term relationships between globalization and social progress can only be hypothesized. Therefore, the analysis presented in this part of the study should be treated with caution.

Notwithstanding these caveats, theoretical considerations and empirical evidence suggest that globalization has the potential to increase peoples' welfare. As numerous studies and historical data show, trade and FDI liberalization lead to high economic growth, while, conversely, protectionist solutions usually have a negative effect on living standards.[1] Most cross-country studies conclude that increased trade and FDI flows can, at least in the long run, be correlated with higher rates of economic growth and productivity increases for the economy as a whole.[2]

The potential gains are, however, neither automatic nor painless. They depend on initial conditions, external economic developments and policies. For the benefits to materialize, some adjustments are inevitable, which, almost by definition, involve intersectoral flows of employment and related adjustments costs for displaced workers. Even beyond these transitory costs, globalization can entail long-lasting effects on earnings and incomes of different groups, resulting in wider income inequalities. Some individuals or groups may benefit more than others: for example, skilled as opposed to unskilled workers (as in Switzerland) or urban vis-à-vis rural areas (as appears to be the case in Bangladesh and Poland).

There is probably also a link between globalization, on the one hand, and economic and labour market insecurity, on the other. As markets become more global, even well-established enterprises are being challenged, which may produce a feeling of insecurity among the workers and employers concerned. Furthermore, it has become technically possible to outsource parts of the production process to other countries, which may also threaten job security. More fundamentally, comparative advantage is increasingly subject to change, to the extent that some observers have coined the term "kaleidoscopic comparative advantage" – cross-country analysis carried out by the ILO Task Force confirms that the more open the economy, the more intersectoral employment flows can be observed (see below). Globalization is also associated with the erosion of the standard "Fordist" model of salaried employment. New forms of employment are emerging, and, although these non-standard forms in many cases correspond to new options for many workers, there is justified concern about their negative social consequences, in particular for the low skilled. These issues are addressed in some detail in the following sections.

B. THE COST OF FREE CAPITAL MOVEMENTS

The merits and demerits of free capital movements have been hotly debated over the past few years, particularly since the Asian crisis of 1997–98. Free capital movements have often been advocated by international financial institutions and in certain academic circles (De Long, 1998; Altman, 1998). The main rationale behind this proposal is that freer capital flows should lead to a more efficient allocation of savings across countries. This was believed to be especially beneficial for developing countries, which suffer a chronic shortage of savings, in much the same way as in the 1980s the liberalization of domestic financial markets was regarded as a way of alleviating credit constraints while also improving resource allocation. Many countries have thus embarked on a process of liberalizing their capital accounts.[3]

Liberalization measures have resulted in the build-up of a large stock of financial capital that can move from one country to another almost instantaneously and at limited transaction costs. As a result, national economies have become more vulnerable to the changing perceptions and interests of international investors, to the point that the financial economy may have acquired a certain autonomy with respect to economic fundamentals (and it may even have a negative impact on them). Indeed, it could be argued that there is a real danger that capital flows will increasingly determine exchange rate movements, in turn affecting trade, output and employment levels. By contrast, in the past an opposite causation – running from economic fundamentals to capital flows – was the rule.

Research conducted for this study shows that this may already have happened, at least in the seven emerging market economies for which work was carried out (India, Indonesia, Republic of Korea, Mexico, Philippines, South Africa and Thailand).[4] As table 3 shows, in the 1980s movements in the real exchange rate in one particular quarter were often caused by developments in the basic balance of payments in the previous quarter (i.e. the current account ·

Table 3 Correlation between capital flows and real exchange rates of selected countries, 1981–98

Country	Correlation between financial capital flows in one quarter and real exchange rates in the following quarter		Correlation between the "basic" balance of payments in one quarter and real exchange rates in the following quarter	
	1981Q1 to 1989Q4	1990Q1 to 1998Q4	1981Q1 to 1989Q4	1990Q1 to 998Q4
India	−0.0	+0.3*	+0.0	+0.2
Indonesia	−0.1	+0.6*	+0.6*	+0.0
Korea, Republic	−0.3	+0.5*	+0.7*	+0.1
Mexico	−0.2	+0.1	+0.5*	+0.3*
Philippines	−0.1	+0.3	+0.1	+0.3*
South Africa	−0.3	+0.0	+0.4*	+0.1
Thailand	−0.0	+0.2	+0.3*	+0.1

Note: The table shows correlation coefficients based on quarterly data, with an asterisk (*) denoting that the coefficient is significant at the 10 per cent level. Financial capital flows include net portfolio investments, investments (excluding FDI) by banks and other private agents, and errors and omissions. The "basic" balance of payments is the current account balance plus net FDI flows.

Source: ILO Task Force estimates, based on IMF (1999).

balance plus net FDI flows). A positive basic balance exerted appreciating pressure on the currency, and conversely in the case of a basic balance deficit. As expected, the correlation coefficients shown in the table are relatively high and statistically significant in five out of seven cases. This causality almost completely disappeared in the 1990s, when correlation coefficients became small and insignificant, with the possible exceptions of Mexico and the Philippines. While the basic balance of payments plays less of a role in exchange rate determination, private capital flows have become an important determining factor; during the 1980s there was no significant causal link between net private capital flows in one particular quarter and real exchange movements in the following quarter, whereas this appeared to be the case in the 1990s, as illustrated by the fact that correlation coefficients increased and several were statistically significant.

The instability of short-term capital flows has triggered a debate on how they should be controlled. In this respect, it is useful to look at the Chile country study. In Chile, capital flows had also been slightly liberalized, but certain restrictions were maintained in the form of non-remunerated reserve requirements. Thus, despite the difficulties of controlling short-term capital flows (investors quickly learn to circumvent existing control measures, which means that authorities are forever on the look-out for new mechanisms), the Government of Chile managed to avoid an excessive volatility of capital flows (Reinecke and Torres, 2001). It should also be stressed that Chile's current account deficit, a reflection of the country's high domestic investment rate, has been financed mainly by long-term capital inflows. Somewhat paradoxically, though, reserve requirements were removed by the Central Bank of Chile precisely at the time that public discussion was centring on the advantages of having some form of restriction on short-term capital flows. In this discussion, Chile's regulations were seen as one possible model of transparent and well-administered control.

C. GLOBALIZATION AND INCOME INEQUALITIES

According to standard economic theory, under certain conditions international trade should help diminish income inequalities in developing countries and threaten to increase inequalities in industrialized countries. Compared with industrialized countries, developing economies have relatively abundant unskilled labour, for which the demand is likely to grow as trade flows between developing and industrialized countries intensify. This, in turn, should raise the wages of unskilled workers relative to those of skilled workers, thereby diminishing income inequalities. Theoretically at least, the opposite would be expected to occur in industrialized countries. But empirical evidence suggests that the direct impact of trade on income inequalities is small. Furthermore, trade seems to be associated with wider income inequalities in developing as well as in developed countries, which is at variance with conventional theory. In fact, what seems to be at work here is the effect of skill-based technological change.

The impact of trade on labour markets also depends on the nature of international specialization. The ILO Task Force's study on Switzerland provides evidence that import penetration is associated with reduced wages mainly in industries producing relatively homogeneous products, such as textiles. But where competition takes place mainly through export differentiation (as in the mechanical and engineering industries), there is no evidence that trade leads to a decline in wages. To the extent that niche industries have a higher intensity of skilled labour than those that make homogeneous goods, trade can, therefore, contribute to widening income inequalities (Romero and Torres, 2001; figure 5).

The evidence concerning the emerging and developing countries studied by the ILO Task Force shows that international trade has tended to be associated with wider income inequalities (table 4). In Chile and Bangladesh, income inequalities grew during the trade liberalization process. Widening income inequality in Bangladesh has led to a stagnation of the incomes of the poorest households, despite sizeable increases in average household incomes (figure 6). This is

Figure 5   Switzerland: Labour market characteristics of the country's industrial
           specialization, 1994

A. Composition of exports and imports by level of product differentiation

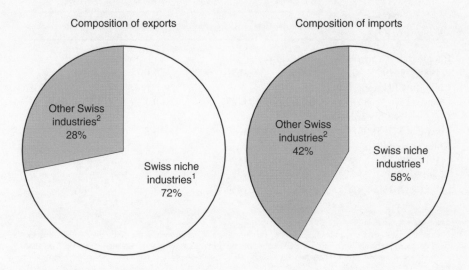

B. Labour market characteristics of industrial activities (low-differentiated/
   homogeneous and differentiated products)

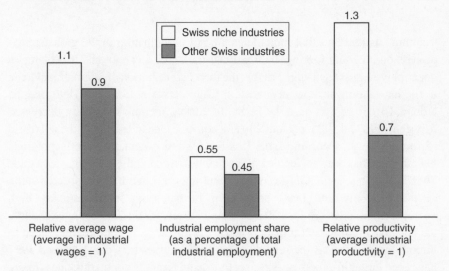

[1] Niche industries: differentiated products (food, drinks and tobacco, chemicals, machinery and electronics, watches and jewellery).   [2] Other industries: low-product differentiation (textiles, apparel, wood, paper, printing, shoes and leather, rubber and plastic products, non-metallic minerals, metals, other manufacturing goods).

Source: Romero and Torres (2001).

Table 4 Household income distribution before and after trade liberalization, various years

Country and years[1]	Gini coefficient		Ratio of income dispersion[2]	
	Pre-liberalization	Post-liberalization	Pre-liberalization	Post-liberalization
Bangladesh (1988–89, 1995–96)	0.28	0.31	7.0	8.8
Chile, first liberalization phase (1970, 1980)[3]	0.43	0.47	9.1	10.6
Chile, second liberalization phase (1987, 1996)	n.a.	n.a.	13.3	13.8
Korea, Republic of (1985, 1997)	0.35	0.29	n.a.	n.a.
Mauritius (1986–87, 1996–97)	0.40	0.39	7.8	7.6

n.a. = data not available.

[1] The parentheses give the pre-liberalization and post-liberalization years for which the data are presented. Reflecting data availability problems, in the case of Chile's second liberalization phase, the pre-liberalization year is 1987, not 1985. [2] Ratio of income of the 20 per cent richest households to the 20 per cent poorest households. [3] Santiago Metropolitan Region.

Source: ILO Task Force, based on national household surveys.

troubling, as it shows that individuals are not participating in the globalization process on an equal footing. International trade alone cannot take the blame: a quantitative assessment suggests that the direct contribution of international trade to the increase in income inequality in Chile between 1960 and 1996 may be around 10 per cent (figure 7). In South Africa, income inequality decreased between 1990 and 1995, presumably as a consequence of the end of the apartheid regime. However, according to the Task Force's assessment, the net effect of trade liberalization has been a widening of inequalities. Apparently, in South Africa trade liberalization has so far reinforced the capital-intensive international specialization of the economy and there have been further rises in the already high unemployment rates (Hayter, Reinecke and Torres, 2001). Interestingly, though, the negative employment impact of trade liberalization is not directly related to import competition, as the relative employment losses between 1994 and 1997 have been larger in export-oriented sectors than in import-competing ones (figure 8).[5] Studies of other middle-income developing countries, such as Colombia, Costa Rica and Mexico, also conclude that trade liberalization has resulted in increasing income inequalities (Robbins, 1996; Hanson and Harrison, 1995; Wood, 1997).

Figure 6   Bangladesh: Diverging trends in real per capita income of richest and poorest households, 1985–86 to 1995–96 (in Bangladeshi taka)

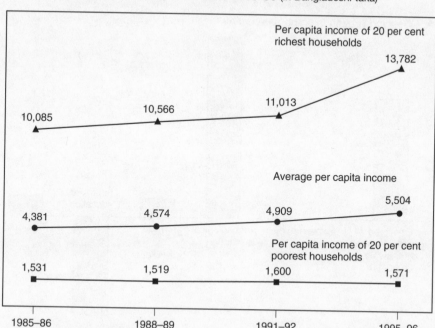

Source: Paratian and Torres (2001).

Poland provides an interesting example of how international trade and FDI often do little to alleviate the problems of depressed areas. In Poland, the international integration of the economy has had a positive effect on trade and FDI, resulting in the emergence of a dynamic private sector, improved living standards and a rise in job opportunities. However, there is evidence that interregional disparities are increasing. The most severely affected areas are the eastern regions (sometimes referred to as "Poland B") and agricultural areas in the east and north, as well as single-industry provinces and towns, which are seeing striking differences in per capita GDP, unemployment rates and the spatial distribution of foreign investment. These regional disparities are reducing the benefits of globalization and hampering the growth process. There is growing awareness in Poland of the need to correct these regional disparities, with the aim of: (a) enhancing the mobility of both labour and capital; (b) strengthening backward linkages; and (c) protecting vulnerable groups.

Two main reasons can be put forward to explain why trade liberalization in many developing countries is increasing the relative demand for skilled workers and reducing the demand for unskilled workers:

27

Figure 7   Chile: Estimated determinants of wage and income inequalities,
1960–96 (as a percentage)

A. Observed growth in wage differentials

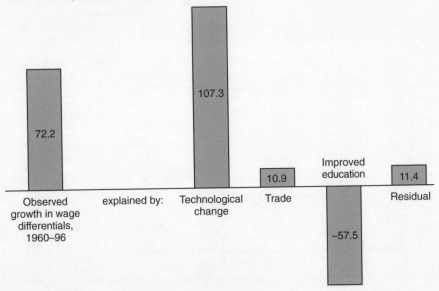

B. Observed growth in household income differentials

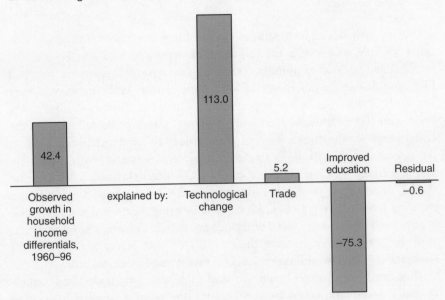

Source: Reinecke and Torres (2001).

Figure 8   South Africa: Labour market performance of manufacturing sectors by trade orientation, 1994–97 (as a percentage of total change)

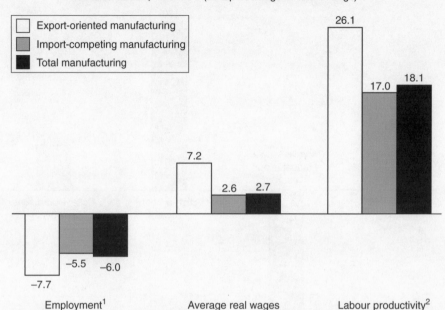

Notes: Revealed comparative advantage is measured as the ratio of net trade flows to total trade (imports plus exports). Manufacturing sectors with a positive revealed comparative advantage in 1997 have been classified as "export-oriented", while those with a negative revealed comparative advantage have been classified as "import-competing".

[1] Employment variation is corrected for the break in January 1996 consecutive to the inclusion of TBVC data for the manufacturing sector. The cumulated variation of employment was calculated from a composite of employment variation from 1994 to December 1995 and employment variation from January 1996 to 1997. [2] Labour productivity is calculated as gross output per employed person

Source: Hayter, Reinecke and Torres (2001).

- The new technologies being introduced in the context of more intensive pressure of international competition tend to require more skilled labour, while the demand for unskilled labour declines.
- Trade liberalization is likely to stimulate the demand for natural-resource-intensive goods, which are relatively abundant in many developing countries. This will benefit the owners of natural resources as well as the earnings of skilled labour, which is more mobile than unskilled labour. By contrast, the earnings of unskilled labour, a factor that is relatively immobile and sector specific, will fall relative to other factors. This is how the exploitation and processing of natural resources can make a country more prone to income inequalities (Reinecke and Torres, 2001).

Figure 9 Republic of Korea: Estimated impact of trade on employment by level of education, 1990 (in thousands)

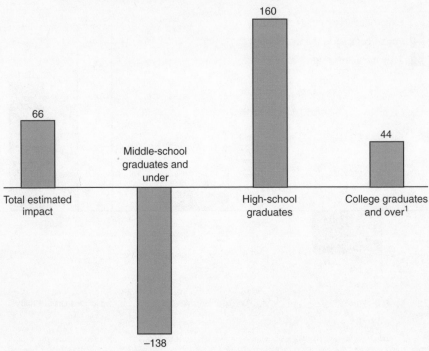

¹ Includes graduates of two-year courses.

Source: Torres (2001).

However, this is certainly not the case in all the countries examined. In Mauritius, export-led growth over the past 15 years has been accompanied by an improvement in income distribution,[6] while in the Republic of Korea income distribution improved until the start of the 1997 crisis. In this country, even though trade is found to have reduced the demand for unskilled labour, the supply-side changes in the form of an upgrading of the labour force have been sufficient to offset the potential negative distributional impact of trade (figure 9). Therefore, strategies aimed at trying to avoid the negative distributional consequences of globalization should focus on the educational upgrading of the labour force (Anker, Paratian and Torres, 2001; Torres, 2001).[7] These results show that the relationship between trade and income inequality can be influenced by the policy setting.

In many developing countries, globalization has been associated with rising women's labour force participation levels. The majority of workers in export-processing zones in Mauritius, for example, are women – 81 per cent in 1983 and 71 per cent in 1995 (Anker, Paratian and Torres, 2001). However, globalization does not seem to have been able to reduce gender-based discrimination: occupational segmentation has not changed decisively, and in many countries women are still over-represented in jobs with relatively low wages, high job insecurity and poor working conditions.

Finally, it is often argued that the increased international mobility of capital has shifted the power balance between capital and labour in favour of capital. As labour in one particular country appears to be relatively easier to replace with labour in other countries, the bargaining position of the workforce may be weakened and a diminishing wage share in GDP can be expected. Indeed, the wage share in GDP has decreased since the 1980s in all but two of the 15 European Union (EU) countries. The result holds true even correcting for the increased number of self-employed workers.[8]

D. GLOBALIZATION AND JOB INSECURITY

In the same way that globalization has an impact on income inequalities, so it exerts pressure on job security – the income and employment effects are two sides of the same coin. Workers can be displaced by competing imports, labour-saving technology and FDI (e.g. through the relocation of certain activities abroad). The increased elasticity of the demand for labour affects mostly low-skilled workers, who tend to have limited mobility and are, therefore, more likely to face high job insecurity (Rodrik, 1997). Globalization is widely considered to be synonymous with shifts in the competitive position of enterprises in world markets and in the position of countries in the international division of labour. These changes inevitably have repercussions at the level of the individual worker, as trade can lead to job creation in industries where comparative advantage lies but to job losses in import-competing industries. Some studies, such as the one conducted by Addison, Fox and Ruhm (1996), suggest that the risk of job loss is highest in sectors that are exposed to import competition.

There is some evidence that job instability is on the rise. Between the 1980s and the 1990s, a widespread, and in some cases quite sharp, increase in individuals' perceptions of job insecurity was observed in most of the Organisation for Economic Co-operation and Development (OECD) countries, including those where the unemployment rate was either relatively low or falling, such as Japan, the United Kingdom and the United States (OECD: *Employment Outlook*, 1997). There is also evidence of higher job turnover in certain countries and for specific segments of the population. In Chile, the rate of job creation and job displacement has grown considerably since the start of trade liberalization and has remained (Reinecke and Torres, 2001).

In other countries an examination of the average job tenure of workers has not yielded any conclusive results: no significant changes in average tenure or gross job flows have been found (ILO, 1996; OECD: *Employment Outlook*, 1997).

Figure 10   Trade and inter-sectoral employment flows, 1986–95 (average incidence
of net inter-sectoral employment changes as a percentage)

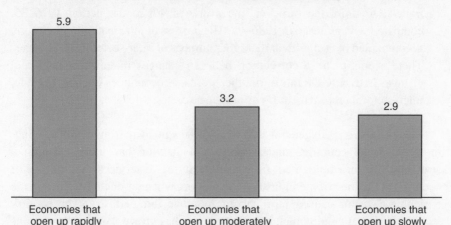

Economies that   Economies that   Economies that
open up rapidly   open up moderately   open up slowly

Notes: The figures refer to the number of workers that move between manufacturing sectors (at 3-digit ISIC level) per
job created in the total manufacturing sector of 77 countries. The higher the figure, the greater the incidence of net inter-
sectoral employment flows. Countries are divided into three groups: the first includes those where the trade/GDP ratio
rises significantly faster than average; the second is those where the change in the trade/GDP ratio comes close to the
international average; countries where trade/GDP ratios grow less than average belong to the last group.

Source: ILO Task Force, based on data from the UNIDO Industrial Statistics Database (1999).

Furthermore, relatively little research has focused on the nature or size of
the adjustment costs associated with trade liberalization. This study attempts to
address this issue, based on the assumption that adjustment costs will be larger,
the greater the difference between job requirements in expanding industries
and job losses in declining industries. When both expanding and declining
industries belong to the same sector, it is usually easier for displaced workers
to find a new job. By contrast, moving into employment in entirely different
sectors is likely to be more difficult, especially for low-educated workers,
whose skills and competencies are often sector specific. Analysis of the
manufacturing employment data of 77 countries (between 1986 and 1995)
conducted for this study[9] suggests that trade is associated with substantial inter-
sectoral labour turnover (and, in this sense, trade is likely to produce relatively
damaging displacement effects). The evidence is as follows:

*   In countries where the trade/GDP ratio has increased faster than the
    international average, the movement of labour between sectors is nearly six
    times larger than the net number of jobs created for the manufacturing
    sector as a whole (figure 10). This is twice as much as in countries where
    the trade/GDP ratio has increased less than the international average.

- Inter-sectoral employment flows have increased in most countries. In countries that have experienced a faster-than-average increase in their trade/GDP ratio, the turnover rate averaged 4.5 in the period 1976–85, compared with almost 6 in 1986–95. The process of job creation is, therefore, accompanied by a significantly higher number of inter-sectoral job changes. There seems to be a correlation between changes in turnover rates and changes in trade/GDP ratios. In other words, as economies open up to trade, inter-sectoral employment flows tend to rise.

There is also a more general shift of employment away from manufacturing: in most of the countries under study, globalization has translated into a structural shift in employment from manufacturing to services. A similar shift occurred at the time of the Industrial Revolution, when productivity gains in the agricultural sector caused farm labour to move into industry. The country studies show that employment in export sectors has grown, but that these gains have not compensated for the losses recorded in import-competing sectors. The reason is that substantial productivity gains have occurred in manufacturing taken as a whole, and these gains have translated into lower relative industrial prices, so that the gains have gone to consumers: in other words, industrial goods have become cheaper. Instead of buying more of these goods, however, consumers have tended to demand more services.[10]

E. NEW PATTERNS OF EMPLOYMENT

Up until the 1970s, salaried employment was, either implicitly or explicitly, based on the model of a "standard" employment relationship, with the following characteristics: one lifetime employer and workplace; an indefinite work contract; full-time work; and some degree of social and legal protection.

Although even during the 1970s this standard employment relationship was far from universal (especially in many developing countries), the last few years have seen a rise in non-standard or atypical forms of work. The lack of comprehensive data and variations in definitions make cross-country comparisons difficult, but analyses of trends within countries and within groups of countries are more reliable. Part-time work has increased since the mid-1970s in most of the countries for which data are available: in the 12 countries that were already EU Member States in 1987, part-time work as a share of total employment rose from 10.7 per cent in 1987 to 11.4 per cent in 1990 and 16.9 per cent in 1997 (table 5). Temporary employment has increased since the mid-1980s in all the sample countries except Japan, where it has remained largely unchanged, and the Republic of Korea, where it has decreased substantially (table 6). In many developing countries, non-standard employment often takes the form of "unprotected" employment, with no written work contract or no legally established social security coverage. Although this kind of "informal" paid work is, of course, not new, available data for a selection of Latin American countries indicate that unprotected salaried employment has increased in all of them since the early 1990s (table 7).

It is difficult to tell whether globalization is responsible for the changes in the patterns of employment, but there are reasons to believe that some correlation exists. As the demand for labour becomes more volatile, non-standard forms of employment can be used by enterprises to increase numerical flexibility (that is, adapting the quantity of labour to rapidly changing and unpredictable requirements). Data for several countries and sectors tend to

Table 5   Part-time work as a share of total employment, mid-1980s to 1998

Country	Mid-1980s	Around 1990	1998 or latest available year
EU-12[1]	10.7 (1987)	11.4 (1990)	16.9 (1997)
Austria	8.4 (1983)	8.8 (1989)	14.9 (1997)
Finland	8.3 (1983)	7.2 (1990)	11.4 (1997)
Sweden	24.8 (1983)	23.2 (1990)	23.8 (1997)
Czech Republic	n.a.	n.a.	5.8 (1998)
Hungary	n.a.	n.a.	3.4 (1998)
Norway	29.0 (1983)	26.6 (1990)	26.5 (1997)
Poland	n.a.	10.7 (1992)	10.4 (1998)
Slovenia	n.a.	n.a.	1.7 (1995)
Switzerland	n.a.	24.4 (1991)	28.3 (1997)
Turkey	n.a.	9.2 (1990)	6.2 (1998)
Australia	17.5 (1983)	21.6 (1990)	25.1 (1997)
Canada	16.8 (1983)	17.0 (1990)	19.0 (1997)
United States	18.4 (1983)	17.3 (1990)	16.9 (1998)
Israel	28.1 (1987)	29.3 (1990)	25.8 (1996)
Japan	16.2 (1983)	19.1 (1990)	23.6 (1998)
Korea, Republic of	n.a.	4.5 (1990)	6.8 (1998)
New Zealand	15.3 (1983)	18.8 (1990)	23.7 (1998)
Singapore	n.a.	n.a.	3.3 (1997)
Argentina	17.6 (1987)	n.a.	n.a.
Mexico	n.a.	n.a.	15.0 (1998)
Mauritius	n.a.	n.a.	11.7 (1995)

n.a. = data not available
[1] Belgium, Denmark, France, Germany, Greece, Ireland, Italy, Luxembourg, Netherlands, Portugal, Spain and the United Kingdom.

Sources: ILO (various years); OECD (various years); Eurostat (various years); and national labour surveys.

confirm the link between non-standard employment and globalization. Some enterprises in South Africa, for example, have reacted to increased competitive pressure by turning dependent workers into "independent contractors" (Hayter, Reinecke and Torres, 2001). In Chile, over 90 per cent of the jobs in export-oriented agricultural activities are temporary, while the proportion is 55 per cent in import-competing activities (Reinecke and Torres, 2001). The hiring of large numbers of temporary workers appears to be one of the strategies adopted by manufacturing enterprises in Morocco in response to its trade reforms of the 1980s (Currie and Harrison, 1997).

Table 6   Temporary employment as a share of total salaried employment,
            mid-1980s to 1998

	Mid-1980s[2]	Around 1990[3]	1998 or latest available year
EU-12[1]	8.9	10.2	12.2 (1997)
Austria	n.a.	n.a.	7.8 (1997)
Finland	11.2	13.1 (1991)	17.1 (1997)
Sweden	n.a.	9.7	13.5 (1997)
Czech Republic	n.a.	n.a.	7.3 (1998)
Norway	n.a.	n.a.	11.1 (1995)
Poland	n.a.	4.3 (1993)	5.8 (1998)
Turkey	n.a.	5.2	
Australia	21.2	19.3	24.1 (1996)
Canada	n.a.	8.0 (1989)	11.0 (1995)
United States	n.a.	n.a.	14.4 (1996)
Japan	10.5	10.7 (1988)	11.4 (1998)
Korea, Republic of	17.2 (1985)	16.8	14.2 (1998)
The Philippines	n.a.	n.a.	22.3 (1995)
Singapore	n.a.	n.a.	1.9 (1997)
Argentina	n.a.	8.9	10.2 (1996)
Chile	n.a.	n.a.	16.8 (1996)
Colombia	n.a.	15.7	18.0 (1996)
Peru	n.a.	29.4 (1989)	55.3 (1996)

n.a. = data not available

Notes: Argentina, Chile, Colombia and Peru: Data refer to workers with written work contracts only. Korea, Republic of: Temporary employment refers to daily workers. Peru: Data refer to the industry, construction and services sectors. The Philippines: Temporary employment refers to the categories "short-term", "seasonal" and "working for different employers on a day-to-day or week-to-week basis" as a share of total employment. Singapore: Temporary employment refers to full-time employment only.   United States: Temporary employment refers to contingent workers (individuals who do not perceive themselves as having an explicit or implicit contract for ongoing employment) as a share of total employment.

[1] Belgium, Denmark, France, Germany, Greece, Ireland, Italy, Luxembourg, Netherlands, Portugal, Spain and the United Kingdom. [2] 1987 unless otherwise specified. [3] 1990 unless otherwise specified.

Sources: ILO: *Panorama Laboral* (1997); OECD (various years); Eurostat (various years); Bakkenist Management Consultants (1998); Delsen (1995); Tokman and Martínez (1999) and national labour surveys.

In addition to globalization, developments on the supply side have also contributed to the surge in certain forms of non-standard employment, such as part-time work. As yet, mainly women have opted for this arrangement, as it enables them to combine paid employment with family responsibilities. It is also true that non-standard forms of employment are more frequently found in

Table 7   "Unprotected" salaried employment indicators, early 1990s and 1997
(as a percentage share)

Country	Early 1990s	1997 or latest available year
Argentina	21.7 (1990)	34.0 (1996)
Bolivia	28.0 (1991)	34.8 (1997)
Brazil	31.8 (1992)	32.6 (1997)
Chile	17.0 (1990)	22.3 (1996)
El Salvador	59.1 (1994)	61.3 (1997)
Mexico	43.4 (1990)	49.6 (1997)
Peru	25.5 (1990)	34.1 (1996)

Notes and sources:

Argentina: Private employees without written work contract as a share of total private employment; Greater Buenos Aires, ILO: *Panorama Laboral 1997*, based on data from the Instituto Nacional de Estadística y Censos (INDEC).

Bolivia: Employees not covered by labour and social legislation as a share of total salaried employment, six metropolitan areas: Weller (1998), based on data from the Economic Commission for Latin America and the Caribbean (ECLAC).

Brazil: Private-sector employees *sem carteira* (without a comprensive work contract) as a share of salaried employment; Instituto Brasiliero de Geografia e Estatística (IBGE): *Pesquisa Nacional por Amostra de Domicílios* (various issues).

Chile: Employees without a written work contract as a share of total salaried employment, national; Reinecke and Torres (2001), based on data from the National Socio-Economic (CASEN) survey.

El Salvador: Employed persons not covered by the Instituto Salvadoreño del Seguro Social as a share of total employment, all urban areas: Weller (1998), based on data from ECLAC.

Mexico: Employed without social benefits as a share of total employment, urban areas: Weller (1998), based on data from ECLAC.

Peru: Private employees without a written work contract as a share of total private salaried employment, ILO: *Panorama Laboral* (1997), based on the household survey.

economic sectors not directly exposed to international competition (e.g. non-tradable services).

These results should be interpreted with caution, principally because they do not provide a clear indicator of whether it is globalization in general or trade in particular that causes employment instability. A more quantitative assessment of the correlation is still largely an issue for future research. Moreover, it is possible that workers view inter-sectoral mobility positively and not as a manifestation of job precariousness. The rise in non-standard work does not necessarily mean a higher degree of insecurity. Part-time or temporary work may often be freely chosen. In 1997, for example, 58.5 per cent of part-timers in the 15 EU countries were not looking for a full-time job, and a further 9.5 per cent combined part-time work with school-based education or training. The share of voluntary part-timers was even higher among women (Eurostat: *Labour Force Survey*, 1998). As for temporary work, the share of those people who are voluntarily in this type of employment is much lower. However, for some professionals, such as computer programmers and specialists, temporary employment can sometimes provide better learning and development opportunities than a permanent job with a single employer. And in an environment of rapid domestic and economic and technological change, non-standard forms of employment can, in certain cases, allow for the efficient allocation of labour to activities with higher productivity and, consequently, higher incomes.

On the whole, it seems that, while highly skilled workers often take advantage of non-standard forms of employment, those with lower skills suffer from them. For these low-skilled workers, non-standard forms of employment often mean more vulnerability to economic fluctuations. Legally established rights may not always be respected and collective bargaining may not cover such workers.

It is, therefore, essential to design regulatory frameworks that give a measure of social protection to workers in non-standard forms of employment, where such protection does not already exist. The extension of social insurance mechanisms to these workers is also an important issue.

F. TAXES AND GLOBALIZATION

As mentioned above, globalization can improve business opportunities, thereby raising output and government revenues. On the other hand, it can also affect the tax base in a number of ways. Firstly, implementing trade reforms, whereby significant tariff reductions take place, can impose severe revenue losses on certain countries, particularly developing ones whose trade taxes make up a large share of government revenues. Secondly, partly reflecting capital liberalization and technological change, the mobility of financial capital and businesses, as well as high income groups, has substantially increased. As a result, governments are facing pressure to reduce taxation levels on these mobile production factors. Under these circumstances, governments have to either increase taxation on immobile production factors, such as low-income labour, or reduce expenditure. If the latter option is taken, governments may opt to intensify the fight against "unproductive" public expenditure (which is to be welcomed), although downward pressures on key social protection and education programmes cannot be excluded. Developed countries are better armed to deal with this situation, as they can find tax alternatives more easily than developing countries, where governments often have trouble providing even the most basic of public services.

Trade taxes

Table 8 compares the share of trade taxes in total government revenues between two periods (1976–85 and 1986–95) in three groups of countries – high-, middle- and low-income. Trade taxes include both import duties and export tax revenues. As can be seen, trade taxes declined between the two selected periods for the three groups of countries studied, and the decline is particularly pronounced in the case of low-income countries.

It could be argued that the reduction in trade taxes may have been compensated for by higher revenues from other sources,[11] since governments can

Table 8   Taxes on international trade and government revenues

	Average 1976–85	Average 1986–95	Mean difference	Proportion of countries with negative difference (%)
Taxes on international trade (% of current revenues)				
Low-income countries (31)[1]	34.1	28.6	–5.5	74.2
Middle-income countries (54)	23.7	19.3	–4.3	61.1
High-income countries (31)	8.3	6.4	–1.8	83.9
Total tax revenues (% of GDP)				
Low-income countries (32)	14.3	13.3	–1.0	53.1
Middle-income countries (53)	19.3	20.6	+1.3	43.4
High-income countries (28)	25.6	27.5	+1.9	17.9
Trade (% of GDP)				
Low-income countries (50)	59.9	64.3	+4.4	46.0
Middle-income countries (61)	84.7	89.1	+4.4	37.7
High-income countries (29)	87.1	87.5	+0.4	55.2

Note: The per capita income threshold levels for the three categories are those of the World Bank in 1996: low-income countries have a gross national product per capita (in 1996) of US$785 or less; middle-income countries are in the range US$786–US$9,635; and high-income countries are above US$9,635.

[1] The total number of countries with usable observations is given in parentheses.

Source: ILO Task Force, based on 1997 *World Bank Development Indicators* CD-ROM.

compensate for the losses in revenue by either increasing other types of taxes or by collecting more revenue from the higher output that presumably arises from trade liberalization. There is some evidence to support this argument in the case of middle-income and developed countries. Indeed, as shown in table 8, total government revenues as a percentage of GDP have increased in parallel with the reduction in trade taxes. However, the opposite trend can be observed in developing countries, suggesting that trade liberalization may have eroded the tax base and, other things being equal, affected the capacity of these countries to fund social programmes. Certainly, in the face of lower tax revenues, authorities need to intensify their efforts to reduce unproductive public spending and waste, including in the area of social safety net programmes. But, in practice, a cut in essential social protection services cannot be ruled out, so that the tax effects of globalization will often add downward pressure on these services, at least in developing countries.

Taxation on revenues of high-income individuals

In both developed and middle-income countries, the reduction in trade taxes has been accompanied by higher revenues from other sources. It could, therefore, be argued that trade liberalization has not affected the tax base in these countries. However, important distributive effects may have been at work in this process, especially taking into account evidence of an almost universal reduction in taxation on high earners. Practically all developed countries have seen a significant reduction in the top marginal rate of income tax (figure 11A); in the case of middle-income and developing countries, the drop has been even more spectacular (figures 11B and 11C).

To some extent, the reduction in these taxes has been part of a deliberate attempt by governments to encourage individuals to work, save and invest. In this sense, some observers have argued that such a reform may be in the interest of society. Indeed, there is no simple relationship between tax rates and revenues, and lower tax rates can lead to higher or lower fiscal revenues depending on a variety of factors, such as the impact of tax reforms on economic growth. Nevertheless, it should be noted that taxes on middle and low incomes, social contributions and indirect taxes have tended to stabilize or even to increase, so that the drastic reduction in top marginal income taxes has conceivably had a negative impact on income distribution.

One cannot ignore the trade-off that governments must face when confronted with increasing economic integration. On the one hand, tariffs and taxes in general can introduce distortions in consumption and production patterns in the economy, with concomitant welfare costs. On the other hand, the removal of these taxes implies revenue losses for the authorities, as well as a reduced autonomy in implementing policies. As acknowledged by Tanzi (1995), diminished fiscal revenues may be deplored or welcomed, depending on society's preferences regarding the size of the government and its degree of intervention in the economy. This is one reason why all social groups should have a voice.

Among the countries examined, the trade-off between reducing tax rates and strengthening basic public services is best illustrated by Poland. As the study shows, the development of Poland's physical infrastructure and its human capital are two of the country's major policy priorities (Torres et al., 2001). Action in these areas would enhance the benefits of globalization and strengthen the economic sustainability of Poland's expansion phase, while also contributing to reducing regional disparities. It might also help absorb the high levels of "hidden" unemployment in the Polish agricultural sector. Obviously, this would have an effect on government spending. Even though there is scope for improving public-sector efficiency and reducing expenditure in non-priority

Figure 11   Top marginal tax rate on individual incomes, 1986 and 1998

A. Selected high-income countries and territories

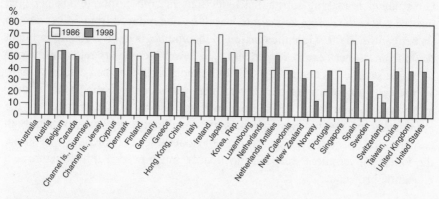

B. Selected middle-income countries and territories

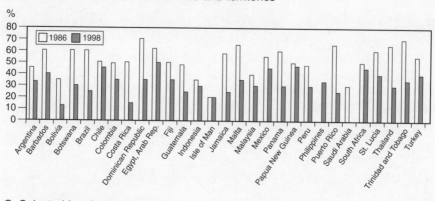

C. Selected low-income countries

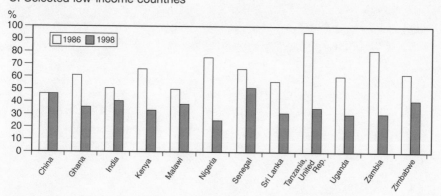

Sources: ILO Task Force, based on Coopers & Lybrand: *1986 International Tax Summaries, A Guide for Planning and Decisions* (New York, John Wiley & Sons, 1986); and PricewaterhouseCoopers: *Individual Taxes 1998, Worldwide Summaries, 1998.*

areas, bringing the infrastructure and education systems of the country closer to EU standards is likely to increase government spending. At the same time, the Government is making substantial reductions in both corporate and personal income taxes: the corporate tax rate was due to be reduced from 34 per cent to 28 per cent in 2000, while the maximum income tax is to be gradually brought down from 40 per cent to 28 per cent. The lower income tax rate, however, is to be left practically unaltered – it is to be reduced by one percentage point to 18 per cent. According to the Government, these changes should not unduly affect government revenues, because they are due to be accompanied by the elimination of many tax deductions that made the previous system both complex and opaque. Even so, it is possible that these tax reductions will hinder the Polish Government's capacity to finance much-needed infrastructure and education projects.

G. THE MULTILATERAL TRADE LIBERALIZATION PROCESS AND DEVELOPING COUNTRIES

The Final Act of the Uruguay Round of multilateral trade negotiations, signed in April 1994, was hailed as a historic event for a number of reasons. Firstly, for its length: it was the longest trade negotiation ever, having begun in 1986. Secondly, the high participation rate of developing countries had a bearing on its agenda and was a determining factor in formulating the rules of the new trading system. Thirdly, wider coverage of new areas such as services, intellectual property rights and investment measures was achieved. Moreover, a programme for agricultural trade liberalization and the full integration of trade in textiles and clothing within the General Agreement on Tariffs and Trade (GATT) framework of rules was introduced. The agreement led to the creation of the WTO, the organization responsible for strengthening the rule of law governing international trade and ensuring its application through an effective, integrated, dispute-settlement mechanism consolidated by more transparent and stringent rules. The Final Act has also contributed to the reduction of tariffs on manufactured products, and the gradual phasing-out of the Multifibre Arrangement and voluntary export restraints, as well as the rolling back of non-tariff measures. In this context, several influential studies published in the early 1990s predicted the advent of a period of high growth, which would translate into an additional increase in world output and living standards worth hundreds of billions of dollars.

Today, the process of trade liberalization is unquestioned: none of the countries studied here has considered returning to less liberal trade practices. Even so, concern has been expressed about the effects of the Uruguay Round agreement, notably its implications for developing countries, which now represent three-quarters of WTO membership (from a total of 131 members), compared with two-thirds in 1982. Although these countries account for one-fifth of world exports, compared with one-tenth in 1982 (World Bank, 1998; WTO, 1998), several problems exist regarding their participation in the multilateral system and the socio-economic implications of the trade agreements:

- For small and low-income countries, effective participation in the WTO's activities remains a serious problem, especially in view of the increasing complexity and range of issues handled by the organization. This raises difficult technical and institutional problems for these countries.
- Before the conclusion of the Uruguay Round, developing countries tended to rely on relatively high tariff and non-tariff barriers. The agreement, therefore, indicates that these countries will have to make a supreme effort to fulfil the new trading rules, even after special and differentiated treatment has been granted to them (e.g. these countries are often given more time to implement the agreement than developed ones).
- Trade liberalization tends to increase export specialization, which, in the case of certain developing countries, might translate into a heavy reliance on a small range of export products. Although development prospects generally do not depend on the number of products exported, a narrow export base can increase economic and labour market vulnerabilities to terms-of-trade shocks.
- Developing countries often specialize in markets subject to fierce pressures in terms of price and cost, such as textiles and raw materials. As a result, these countries are more vulnerable to fluctuations in exchange rates and sudden international changes in wages and prices. By contrast, developed countries tend to specialize in the trade of relatively differentiated products, for which competition takes place mainly in the form of quality changes and innovation (see the Switzerland case study; Romero and Torres, 2001). Such patterns of specialization greatly help cushion countries against external shocks.
- The elimination or reform of certain arrangements, such as the Multifibre Arrangement and the Lomé Convention, can be problematic for countries used to enjoying privileged access to the markets of developed countries.

In this context, a number of initiatives have been taken to help the least-developed countries (LDCs) integrate internationally. For example, in collaboration with UNCTAD, the United Kingdom is supporting projects to train officials of the trade and environment departments of developing countries. Also, since the establishment of the WTO in 1995, technical cooperation activities (such as missions and seminars) of the WTO Secretariat have dramatically expanded, made possible by extra-budgetary contributions from a number of WTO members to the Technical Cooperation Trust Fund. In 1999 alone, more than 380 missions and seminars took place, with the aim of improving the participation of the developing countries in the WTO system. The LDCs and the African countries received particular attention: more than 130 technical cooperation activities were directed to their needs.

Similarly, in 1997 the Commonwealth of Nations set up a Trade and Investment Access Facility, which, among other functions, funds capacity-building in the field of the legal implementation of the WTO Agreements. In 1998, the Commonwealth Secretariat set up a joint Task Force on Small States with the World Bank, at the request of the Commonwealth Heads of Government at their meeting in Edinburgh, Scotland, in 1997, where the strategic concerns of small States were examined. The first meeting of the Joint Task Force took place in Washington, DC, on 8 October 1998. The main objectives of the Task Force were to "analyse the implications for small States of recent significant changes in the global economy and regimes governing international trade, propose ways of overcoming problems (in terms of what the EU, WTO and other organizations might be asked to do) and set out measures that will enable small States to take advantage of opportunities created by these developments" (Commonwealth Secretariat, 1998). The Commonwealth Secretariat published its final report, *The trade implications for small vulnerable States of the global trade regime shift*, in December 1998. The Joint Commonwealth Secretariat/World Bank Task Force held its second meeting in St Lucia in the Caribbean in February 1999, where it discussed, among other issues, the first draft of the report, *Small States: A composite vulnerability index*.

Under the WTO Agreement, it is stipulated that the LDCs recognized as such by the United Nations will only be required to undertake commitments and concessions that are consistent with their individual development, financial and trade needs or their administrative and institutional capabilities. In line with the Agreement governing the structure of the WTO – which recognizes that there is a need for positive efforts designed to ensure that developing countries, and especially the least developed among them, secure a share in the growth of international trade commensurate with their economic development needs – the General Council established the WTO Committee on Trade and Development on 31 January 1995, which, in turn, established the WTO Sub-Committee on Least-Developed Countries on 5 July 1995. The WTO is holding consultations with its member governments on a package of market-access measures to help the LDCs increase their participation in world trade. The WTO's efforts focus on providing LDC governments with duty-free, quota-free market access to their main export markets. Main importers, including Canada, the EU, Japan and the United States, are also studying various options. LDC governments have also called on their industrialized trading partners to eliminate all export subsidies – within an agreed time frame – on all agricultural products of export interest to LDCs.

Important as they are, these efforts do not fully integrate the concerns of developing countries, in particular from the point of view of the socio-economic implications of the trade liberalization process. The risk is that, in the absence of a more proactive approach, social support for trade liberalization in developing countries will be undermined. This would be detrimental to all economies, at all stages of development, all the more so because developing countries could become the main engine of the world economy. This is why, at the last meeting of the ILO Working Party on the Social Dimensions of the Liberalization of International Trade, the government representative of Bangladesh suggested that a globalization fund be set up, an issue that the ILO could explore further.

Notes

[1] For a comprehensive study on the effects of trade liberalization, see OECD (1998).

[2] For example, Edwards (1998), using comparative data for 93 countries and different openness indicators, finds that more "open" countries have experienced faster total factor productivity (TFP) growth and that this result is robust to the use of openness indicator, estimation technique, time period and functional form. On the link between FDI and economic growth, see de Mello (1997); Borensztein, de Gregorio and Lee (1995).

[3] For example, reflecting the wider access of Korean firms and banks to foreign loans, the total foreign debt of the Republic of Korea doubled between 1993 and 1997 to over US$140 billion – about 90 per cent of the total exports of goods and services, or US$3,000 per Korean inhabitant (Torres, 2001).

[4] Owing to lack of data, it was not possible to extend this research to other emerging economies.

[5] Econometric estimates have confirmed the absence of any direct link between increased import penetration in manufacturing sectors and relative employment losses in South Africa (Hayter, Reinecke and Torres, 2001).

[6] This may be because Mauritius has a relatively developed social security system.

[7] Since the start of the crisis, however, income inequalities have deteriorated in the Republic of Korea.

[8] The average wage share for the EU was 73.2 per cent for the period 1981 to 1990, but only 68.3 per cent in 1998. There was also a decline in the wage share in Japan during the same period (from 75.1 per cent to 72.7 per cent), while the United States saw a slight increase – from 71.6 per cent to 72.4 per cent (European Commission, 1998).

[9] This analysis is based on data from the United Nations Industrial Development Organization (UNIDO). The use of net employment flows between sectors is not an optimal indicator of displacement and adjustment costs. Employment flows can occur in both directions and the number of concerned workers (gross employment flows) is, therefore, higher. However, no consistent set of data on gross employment flows in a sufficiently large number of sample countries was available during the course of the project.

[10] Indeed, the income elasticity of the demand for services is usually greater than unity.

[11] The removal of non-tariff barriers generally translates into higher tax revenues – to the extent that imports subject to these barriers are taxed. Likewise, the elimination of import tariff exemptions usually makes room for higher tax revenues. Therefore, certain aspects of trade liberalization can raise revenues.

PART III

THE ROLE OF POLICIES

The findings described above suggest that globalization can lead to new business opportunities and therefore better economic prospects, but that it can also entail considerable adjustment costs and risks of wider income inequalities and increased job insecurity. There is growing concern about employment stability as firms adjust to the pressures arising from greater international competition. Some enterprises are well placed to gain from this process, while others may be worse off in either relative or absolute terms, However, none of the countries studied has considered protectionist measures with respect to trade and FDI as a solution to these problems. Instead, the challenge seems to lie in selecting the appropriate mix of measures (by governments and the social partners) to improve the returns from globalization while reducing the social costs. The country studies show that, in contrast to the view that national governments are powerless in the face of globalization, domestic policies can have a strong bearing on the relationship between globalization and social progress.

A. ENHANCING BUSINESS OPPORTUNITIES ARISING FROM GLOBALIZATION

All too often, the employment debate focuses almost exclusively on the issue of labour market reform. For example, it is sometimes argued that greater labour market flexibility can help increase the employment content of economic growth. Leaving aside the ambiguity of the term "flexibility", it is somewhat surprising that relatively little attention has been devoted to the issue of how product-market reforms can help improve employment prospects. The policy thinking around globalization is no exception: it often ignores the fact that, for new business opportunities created by trade and FDI liberalization to materialize, an environment must exist in which individuals can innovate and create new enterprises for which there is also an appropriate product market.

Trade liberalization raises the profitability of export sectors, creating room for increasing output and employment in those sectors. This provides fertile ground for expanding capacity in existing firms, attracting foreign companies or creating entirely new businesses. However, the presence of internal competition barriers, such as cartel-type arrangements between incumbent firms, will weaken the effects of these favourable conditions. In the words of a recent paper by the South African Department of Trade and Industry: "The elimination of trade and investment barriers may only be a necessary and not a sufficient condition for ensuring that markets are genuinely contestable. What liberalization may grant, restrictive business practices may deny. The concentration of South Africa's industrial sectors has already been identified as one of the key inhibitors to foreign direct investment" (cited in Hayter, Reinecke and Torres, 2001).

Import liberalization hits import-competing sectors when imported goods compete with domestic production. But the process will also reduce import prices and, at the same rate, raise consumers' real incomes. Given the relatively high consumption propensity for services, the real income gains so realized are often spent on services. In other words, import liberalization tends to raise the demand for domestic, often non-tradable, services. Therefore, creating a favourable competitive environment for the delivery of services is probably a key factor in improving the effects of globalization. Establishing a propitious environment for enterprise creation is considered in all of the country studies.

The role of banks as intermediaries also comes into play. The extent to which credit is allocated efficiently will shape firms' responses to globalization. It is interesting to note in this respect that the Government of the Republic of Korea and the social partners have identified the ties between big conglomerates (known as *chaebol*) and banks as an important factor behind the recent financial crisis. Some *chaebol* believed that they could be bailed out by commercial banks and, if necessary, the Government. This "too big to fail" mentality had apparently encouraged risky investments on the part of these groups. The Government, in consultation with the social partners, has now undertaken important reforms regarding this issue. Thus, in 1999 the *chaebol* were compelled, for the first time, to submit consolidated financial statements to the authorities. In the same spirit, management responsibilities in the case of management failure are to be clarified. In order to strengthen the rights of minority shareholders, listed corporations will now have to appoint external directors. Also, intra-group debt guarantees are being phased out, the intention being to reduce the ties between different parts of the conglomerates.

In the case of Bangladesh, the financial sector is handicapped by weak institutional capabilities, a fragmented and ineffectual regulatory framework, and a lack of skilled staff. Commercial banks are saddled with sizeable non-performing assets, which seem to reflect inefficiencies in their role as intermediaries. But this problem is not insurmountable, as has been illustrated by the formation, over the past 15 years or so, of a large number of banks specializing in loans to poor individuals. They have been particularly successful, and have encouraged new initiatives among disadvantaged groups. The unique example of the Grameen Bank in Bangladesh and its performance record in micro-credit delivery to the poor is a case in point. With an average loan size slightly above US$100, the borrowers, often women, are able to set themselves up in self-employment. In this way, the bank claims that 54 per cent of Grameen's borrowers have crossed the poverty line (Paratian and Torres, 2001).

In short, removing the barriers to innovation and enterprise creation, combined with efforts to ensure that the financial sector intermediates on the basis of commercial criteria, can play a key role in enhancing the benefits of globalization. Furthermore, these policies can also serve social objectives. South Africa's competition policy, for example, controls the concentration of economic power, referred to as "public interest considerations" (Hayter, Reinecke and Torres, 2001). In Switzerland, access to high-income professions

– such as medicine and law – has for long been restricted. However, following a comprehensive government programme in the field of competition policy, entry into these professions should now become progressively easier, thereby contributing to job creation and a more equitable distribution of income (Romero and Torres, 2001).

B. STRENGTHENING THE FOUR SOCIAL PILLARS

Policy analyses in individual countries show that action taken in the areas of the labour market and social safety nets is not only important in itself – it can also contribute to improving the gains to be made from globalization.

Education and training

There is universal consensus that education and training are an important long-term response to the challenges of globalization. National policies related to the development of human capital have become more important than ever before. There are several economic and social reasons for this. Firstly, education and training have a strong bearing on people's ability to innovate, develop new technologies, improve product marketing, and so on. Secondly, as shown above, one of the engines of globalization – technological change and the adoption of ICT – tends to raise the demand for skilled labour to the detriment of unskilled labour. The increasing hardship that low-skilled workers are enduring in many countries, including those examined by the Task Force, bear testimony to this problem. Thirdly, there is evidence that trade is associated with higher labour market turnover, and that workers whose skills are firm or sector specific (often the low skilled) are likely to suffer more than workers with transferable, general skills. In a context of ever-changing economic conditions, an open economy requires a high degree of professional mobility. Finally, the issue of equal opportunity – notably in access to high-quality education – is a crucial one from the point of view of social equity. Where this is absent, social mobility is extremely difficult for low-income groups. This also has consequences of a political economy nature: when income inequalities widen and feelings of insecurity grow, there is a growing likelihood that a large segment of the population will oppose economic reforms in general and trade liberalization in particular, even though they may not be the main factors at work. Where unequal education opportunities exist, the threat of this happening is, understandably, heightened.

The Republic of Korea, where education has, since the early stages of the country's economic development, become a national priority, is an interesting case in point. Firstly, access to secondary education was opened to everyone in the 1960s and early 1970s, after which substantial efforts were made in tertiary education. Consequently, the enrolment ratio for higher education almost doubled between 1975 and 1980, again more than doubling during the first half of the 1980s. It has continued to rise ever since. The enrolment ratio for higher education rose from 9 per cent in 1970 to 58 per cent in 1995; during the same period the proportion of college graduates in the total population over age 25 increased dramatically from 4.9 per cent to 19.1 per cent. These trends have obviously changed the structure of the labour market. Since 1980, the proportion of college graduates in the labour force has grown from 6.7 to 20.3 per cent, and that of high-school graduates from 21.8 to 42.9 per cent. Conversely, the numbers of middle-school graduates and those with fewer than nine years of schooling have shrunk significantly – the share of these workers in the total labour force has nearly halved to slightly over one-third. The Republic of Korea's educational attainment level is now one of the highest in the world: according to various measures, including the incidence of Bachelor degrees, it outperforms several industrialized countries. Better education has helped reduce the pressure towards labour market inequalities often associated with globalization.

In Switzerland, equal access to a high-quality education and training system is ensured, which partly explains why Swiss firms have specialized in niche and high value added markets. These "niche" markets are characterized by a high degree of product differentiation, which has helped sustain enviably high wages and good working conditions. The Swiss education system is characterized by relatively low drop-out rates, while the dual training system, which combines theoretical classroom courses with practical training and on-the-job experience, has proved to be extremely effective in facilitating the transition from school to work.

Vocational training can help people adapt their skills in the face of ever-changing economic conditions and can also upgrade competencies to meet the challenges of technological change. However, even though its importance is often recognized, getting vocational training off the ground faces substantial obstacles in most, if not all, the countries studied. For instance, the lack of well-qualified staff is one of the major constraints reported by private enterprises in Poland. According to a number of recent surveys, in 1995, 14 per cent of enterprises in Poland identified this as their third most significant difficulty, after lack of funds and limited access to credit. By 1997, 19 per cent of them held that opinion (Eurostat, 1999). When combined with practical work experience in an enterprise, vocational training helps ensure the relevance of training and helps facilitate the transition from school to the workplace. The practice, however, almost ceased in Poland at the beginning of the country's transition period, when many enterprises, concerned more with their own survival in an increasingly competitive environment, gave up running training schemes and lost interest in renewing arrangements for in-house training. In the 1990–91 school year, there were more than 900 vocational schools run by enterprises (they included 29 basic vocational and 227 secondary vocational schools for adults). By 1992, 400 of these schools had been closed down. The Polish Government has now addressed some of these issues through reforms that came into operation in September 1999.

For training to be useful, it must take into account labour market requirements – no easy task. There is always the risk that, once trained in one enterprise, workers will be hired by another firm – the so-called "free-riding" problem, which can be a powerful disincentive to training at the enterprise level.

Social safety nets

A well-functioning social safety net serves two complementary purposes:

- to ensure the fair distribution of the gains and costs associated with globalization and economic restructuring;
- to strengthen workers' support for the reform process. In the absence of a social safety net, workers' opposition to economic restructuring is strong; social safety nets can include unemployment benefits, training programmes for displaced workers and public assistance schemes.

In three of the countries examined – Chile, the Republic of Korea and Poland – the social safety net has recently been strengthened. Chile's participation in the global economy has brought with it a relatively high degree of labour market instability for significant parts of the active population. There is, however, relatively little unemployment protection in Chile, and, as yet, practically no unemployment benefits (moreover, as discussed below, employment protection legislation is relatively lax). As a result, given that many services, such as high-quality healthcare and education, have to be paid for by individuals, even temporary job losses can have a considerable impact on the affected households. A proposal for the introduction of a System of Protection for the Unemployed Worker (PROTRAC), based on individual savings accounts and a joint contribution by employers and workers, is under discussion.

Pensions often provide an element of social protection at a time when job instability is increasing. However, to the extent that pensions are financed by labour taxes, such as social security contributions, they can raise the cost of labour, possibly affecting job creation and reducing the gains to be made from globalization. If pension benefits and contributions are loosely related (as in pay-as-you-earn systems), individuals may have an incentive not to declare their incomes, thereby boosting the "grey" or "informal" economy. The pension system can also either facilitate or deter functional mobility, depending on whether pension benefits are portable between sectors, enterprises and occupations. In several important respects, the pension system that operated in Poland until the end of 1998 was not up to these challenges. Since then, however, Poland's pension system has been reformed in a way that should facilitate a positive response to globalization, even though there remains scope for further action in this area (see box 1).

In the Republic of Korea, the role of the State as a provider of social benefits had, until recently, been modest (except in the case of its national healthcare system). The Korean pension system is, for example, mainly company based. Given the heavy reliance on enterprises to provide benefits, the share of government expenditure on social security and welfare was only 6.1 per cent in 1996, or less than 1 per cent of GDP, extremely low by international standards. Since the start of the Asian crisis, important steps have been taken towards creating a social safety net. In particular, the unemployment benefit system has been reinforced, government support for work-sharing efforts aimed at preventing lay-offs has been made available, company pension rights have been strengthened and the Wage Claim Guarantee Fund has been set up. The adoption of these measures has reduced adjustment costs and lessened opposition to the reform process, thereby contributing to overcome the crisis.

Although the importance of social safety nets is widely recognized, helping low-income groups is no easy task. In addition, it seems that traditional safety nets, such as the family, have been weakened, thereby raising the demand for government support. The case of Mauritius vividly illustrates these emerging problems. In government documents Mauritius is referred to as a welfare State: the country has free education, free health services and a free non-contributory old-age pension for everyone over the age of 60. There are also payments to the disabled, pensioned widows, orphans, destitute families with dependants, unemployed heads of low-income households, and low-income households; furthermore, around one-quarter of all households get food aid, as well as subsidized rice and flour prices. In recent years, social expenditure has accounted for approximately 40 per cent of government expenditure, with education accounting for approximately 17 per cent, health 8 per cent and

Box 1   Pension reform in Poland

Poland's former pension system had long provided adequate coverage for a significant percentage of the population, but at high financial and social costs. Since 1992, expenditure on retirement and disability benefits has consistently exceeded 14 per cent of GDP, that is, more than the EU average (11 per cent) and almost 50 per cent more than in the other Central and Eastern European countries. If reforms had not been introduced, an increase to 22 per cent of GDP by the year 2020 would not have been inconceivable (Góra and Rutkowski, 1998).

The excessive and growing burden of pension expenditure can be explained, in part, by the rapidly growing number of pensioners, the result of an earlier policy that encouraged people to take early retirement (during the first stages of the transition process, early retirement and the granting of disability pensions were widely used to make it easy for people who would otherwise have been unemployed to leave the labour market). But a very high replacement rate also contributed to the growing spending on pensions: in 1996, on average, pension benefits came close to three-quarters of the average wage, an extremely high figure by international comparison. Not only was the system financially unsustainable, but it also, in a number of ways, adversely affected labour costs, functional job mobility and job creation in the formal sector, thereby inhibiting economic and social responses to globalization:

• A mandatory social security contribution amounting to 45 per cent of total wages was in operation.

• The promotion of early retirement dampened some workers' motivation to seek retraining or occupational mobility.

• The farmers' pension fund was, and still is, funded by the State. Consequently, it has been argued that farmers have not had the motivation to seek paid employment outside agriculture or to become self-employed in non-agricultural activities.

• Coverage under the old system was not always adequate, because some employers, in order to avoid paying the full social contributions, either did not declare their workers, or, with their workers' consent, paid contributions based only on the minimum wage, giving an undeclared cash payment to their workers to make up the difference. Such practices contributed to the flourishing grey economy in Poland and also entailed an element of risk for the country's workers – in the event of sickness or accident, workers' entitlements would have been inadequate.

The drawbacks of the old pension system were widely recognized and, in January 1999, a new pension system came into operation. In keeping with the concept that security comes from diversifying the sources of pension income, the new system consists of three pillars. The first, based on the pay-as-you-earn principle, is administered by the new Social Insurance Institute and is financed by retirement insurance contributions. Participation in the scheme is compulsory. The second pillar (open pension funds) is a mandatory earnings-related scheme, but workers can choose the private pension fund in which they place a part of their social security contributions. Both these mandatory pillars are guaranteed by the State and, if a person's combined first- and second-pillar pensions amount to less than the prescribed minimum pension, the difference will be paid out of the state budget. The third pillar is a voluntary supplementary insurance consisting of employer-funded schemes and other saving arrangements. It is designed to encourage employers to contribute to complementary pension plans for their workers, and workers can decide whether or not to participate in it. Finally, the new system radically cuts opportunities for workers to take early retirement.

The new system has several clear advantages over the previous one. It gives incentives to people to declare employment: it is in employees' interest to ensure that their contributions are paid, and they are now more aware of the relationship between the official salary and future pension benefits. In addition, early retirement is expected to become less attractive owing to the cuts in benefits. Also, in order to stimulate workers' interest in alternative employment, some additional new policies have been introduced.

It is still unclear whether the new pension system will lead to a reduction in labour costs. In addition, the separate pension system that covers farmers and agricultural workers has not been reformed. However, the new system is expected to help reduce the pension budget, while at the same time providing an incentive for workers and employers to declare their activities, thereby reducing the incidence of the informal economy. It should eliminate the disincentives to job and occupational stability that characterized the former system and, in so doing, should improve the country's response to globalization.

Source: Torres et al., 2001.

Figure 12   Mauritius: Percentage of government current revenue from
international trade, 1980–97 (as a percentage of current revenue)

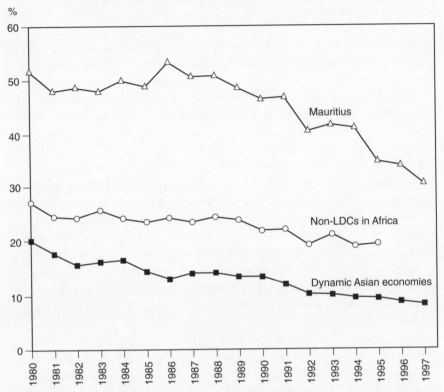

Notes: Dynamic Asian economies include Hong Kong (China), the Republic of Korea, Malaysia, Singapore and Thailand. No data on taxes on international trade are available for Hong Kong (China). Non-LDCs in Africa include Algeria, Botswana, Cameroon, the Congo, Côte d'Ivoire, Egypt, Gabon, Ghana, Kenya, Libyan Arab Jamahiriya, Morocco, Namibia, Nigeria, Senegal, Seychelles, South Africa, Swaziland, Tunisia and Zimbabwe. Totals for dynamic Asian economies and non-LDCs in Africa are unweighted averages.

Source: ILO Task Force, based on data from World Bank: *World Development Indicators* (1999).

social welfare 19 per cent, with non-contributory pensions comprising around 70 per cent of social welfare expenditure. This emphasis is particularly important in a small country with so much ethnic and religious diversity, since good social welfare leads to social cohesion, which means political stability. As stated in a recent official document, it is likely that this concern for social welfare has also contributed to the country's economic development. Despite this positive picture, the country is facing a number of emerging social problems, such as a rising incidence of divorce and suicide, as well as drug addiction and alcoholism.

Another thorny issue is how to help low-income groups while at the same time maintaining the incentive for these groups to participate actively in the labour market. In order to address this issue, in Switzerland the Government has developed a set of active labour market programmes with the aim of maintaining the employability of unemployed individuals. In view of the international debate on the advantages and disadvantages of different support systems, such as negative income tax and the provision of a minimum income, countries have generally opted for rather pragmatic approaches combining work-availability tests, the provision of means-tested benefits and social benefits that make work pay.

Finally, it is sometimes argued that the tax base in many developing countries is too narrow, making it difficult for these economies to create social safety nets. In addition, as already mentioned, the reduction of import tariffs can strongly affect government revenues to the extent that revenues become dependent on import elasticities with respect to price changes. For example, in Mauritius, while taxes on international trade accounted for approximately 52 per cent of government revenue in 1980, by 1996–97 the figure had fallen to 31 per cent (figure 12). In 1995, taxes on international trade accounted for approximately 1 per cent of GDP in developed countries and Singapore, 6 per cent in the Republic of Korea, 12 to 16 per cent in Malaysia and Thailand, and 24 per cent in other non-LDCs in Africa. However, given the fact that globalization acts as a stimulus to growth, other sources of revenue should expand. The rise in real incomes of the richest households that has been observed in most of the countries studied should provide ample room for improving tax revenues. Unfortunately, the trend seems to be towards establishing and/or increasing value added taxes, which are commonly believed to be regressive from the point of view of income distribution.

Labour law and industrial relations

Since globalization exerts pressure on the reallocation of resources across sectors, employment must be sufficiently adaptable to make adjusting easier. The adaptability of employment can be "numerical", meaning that employment levels adjust to changes in demand and output, but it can also be "functional", meaning that employment adjusts through internal redeployment and changes in work organization. At the same time, labour market institutions need to ensure that fundamental workers' rights and labour standards are not undermined. This is important, not only from the point of view of protecting workers, particularly the most vulnerable ones, but also for reasons of economic efficiency: employment stability is often associated with a greater commitment of workers to the firm, while also encouraging training – all factors that contribute to higher productivity gains. There is, of course, a difficult trade-off between numerical and functional adaptability, but international experience suggests that practical solutions to each particular historical and institutional context can usually be found.

In two of the countries studied that have faced a sizeable restructuring challenge – the Republic of Korea and South Africa – labour legislation and regulations have been substantially modified to allow greater scope for the labour force to adjust, while ensuring an adequate degree of workers' protection. In the Republic of Korea, following the reforms of 1997–98, conditions for dismissals were slightly eased. Dismissals for "urgent managerial reasons" were made possible (previously, the law had been extremely restrictive in this respect), with mergers, acquisitions and takeovers now being regarded as included in this category. In all cases, the law requires that every effort has to be made to avoid dismissals. In particular, management should, in consultation with workers' representatives, explore alternatives, such as introducing shorter working hours, stabilizing wages, relocating and retraining. Firms are encouraged to set up committees on working hours to identify ways of stabilizing employment through a reduction in working hours. Moreover, rational and fair standards are required in order to decide which workers to lay off. Furthermore, discrimination on the basis of sex is not permitted. Sixty days prior to carrying out any dismissals, employers have to notify unions or workers' representatives of the alternatives to lay-offs and of the selection procedure for dismissals, and enter into open and sincere discussions with them. Economic conditions permitting, employers should consider re-employing dismissed workers. In South Africa, the Labour Relations Act of 1995 allows for dismissals to be made on fair grounds, such as company restructuring, and requires that they be conducted in a fair manner. In both these countries, it could be argued that action is needed, notably to make sure that employment regulations do not make employers reluctant to create permanent jobs. This raises the issue of how non-permanent (or non-standard) jobs are regulated.

The issue of the regulation of "non-standard" forms of employment, such as the so-called "labour lease" system in the Republic of Korea, contract labour in Chile, on-call work in Switzerland and part-time and fixed-term contracts, is a controversial one. As stressed earlier, these new forms of employment account for a large proportion of the new jobs that have been created over the past few years. They may, in certain cases, be a response to the demands of both enterprises and the individuals concerned. However, in certain contexts they can be subject to abuse and fraud. Countries have tried to deal with this difficult issue in a number of ways:

- Since July 1998, "leased labour" in Korea is subject to certain regulations: previously, no specific legislation existed on this new form of employment.
- According to Chile's Labour Code, an enterprise (the "user enterprise") that uses workers from another enterprise (the "subcontractor") has to pay the wages of the workers and fulfil other social obligations in the eventuality of the subcontractor failing to comply with them. However, non-compliance usually means that workers face a long delay in taking their employers to court.
- New labour legislation in South Africa gives greater scope to employers to renew fixed-term contracts under certain conditions.
- The Polish Government is considering whether to reform the existing legal prohibition on hiring workers for more than two consecutive short-term contracts.

A related issue that arises in most of the country studies but which is of considerably wider relevance is whether collective agreements should be extended to non-parties and, if so, under what conditions. Globalization requires a certain degree of consensus and social dialogue to implement practical solutions. Collective bargaining is an appropriate instrument in this respect, but it cannot take place in certain industries and small enterprises where the union presence is weak. In those sectors and enterprises, should wages and working conditions be set through individual contracts with minimum standards set by national legislation, or should collective agreements reached at the sectoral level be extended to them? In Chile and the Republic of Korea, collective bargaining takes place mainly at the enterprise level; in its absence, minimum wages and standards set by the respective governments have to be applied. In South Africa, collective agreements can be extended to non-parties under certain conditions; non-parties to the agreement, however, can request exemption. In Switzerland, extension is also possible, but conditions are considered to be relatively stringent. Given that there is no national minimum wage in Switzerland, the question has been raised as to whether extension mechanisms should be strengthened in view of the perceived risks of downward pressures on the wages and working conditions of low-skilled workers, which might arise as a consequence of the recently concluded bilateral agreement on the movement of workers between Switzerland and the EU.

Core labour standards

Certain labour standards, termed "core" labour standards, are important from the point of view of the rights they embody. The elimination of child labour, the abolition of forced labour, encouraging non-discrimination in employment, and freedom of association and collective bargaining, embody the rights of all individuals, irrespective of their level of income, sex, race and the political system under which they live. As in the case of other basic rights, core standards entail a responsibility on the part of each individual to respect the rights of other individuals.

The ILO's Declaration on Fundamental Principles and Rights at Work and its Follow-up provides the framework to move forward on this issue. The fact that all ILO member States have endorsed the Declaration illustrates the universal nature of these standards. It is also important for the success of the promotional nature of the Declaration that member States understand that it is in their own interest to enforce core labour standards. Indeed, the enforcement of core standards can influence economic development generally, and trade in particular, through a variety of channels (OECD, 1996; Torres, 2000):

- Core standards form framework conditions for an efficient allocation of resources – that is, they prepare the ground for the efficient operation of market forces.
- In certain cases, they can help create an environment conducive to stable labour/management relations and human capital accumulation, with positive externalities on productivity gains.
- They enhance social equity and, in doing so, ensure that the distribution of the gains from economic growth and trade liberalization are shared fairly and impartially.
- Respect for core standards strengthens society's support for market-oriented and open-trade policies.

Child labour is detrimental to development, since it means that the next generation of workers will be unskilled and less well educated. In today's increasingly globalized economy, this has especially negative consequences, since, as pointed out in this report, a skilled and educated labour force is critical to economic development, increasing incomes and social progress. Likewise, the right to organize and bargain collectively is an essential element of success in the global economy. Trade unions, collective bargaining and tripartite dialogue are necessary elements for creating an environment that encourages innovation and higher productivity, attracts FDI and enables societies and economies to adjust to external shocks, such as financial crises and natural disasters. Finally, the discrimination faced by women and minority groups is an important obstacle to economic efficiency and social development. When more than half of a country's potential workforce is inefficiently used, it is inevitable that international competitiveness will be negatively affected.

It is difficult to discern a strong empirical link across countries between the degree of enforcement of core standards, on the one hand, and economic and trade performance, on the other. If anything, it would seem that the relationship is a mutually reinforcing one. As shown in the country studies, the forces associated with globalization and trade liberalization have increased the importance of core standards. The country studies carried out by the Task Force provide information on and analysis of three of the four fundamental rights covered by the ILO's Declaration on Fundamental Principles and Rights at Work and its Follow-up (only forced or compulsory labour was not covered, as it is not a significant issue in the countries examined). Where relevant, the position of the core standards has been documented in the studies, and analyses undertaken as to how the observance of these fundamental rights contributes to both development and international competitiveness.

The Bangladesh garment industry provides an interesting example of the fight against child labour. In order to deal with this situation, the Bangladesh Garment Manufacturers' Association concluded a Memorandum of Understanding for the elimination of child labour in the industry. This shows how child labour can be eliminated from specific export industries without harming the children financially, although it must be admitted that industry-specific programmes do not address the problem of child labour in its entirety.

In all the country studies, information on industrial relations and union density rates were collected. Several of them provide evidence of the constructive roles that the social partners have played in promoting economic development, as follows:

- In the Republic of Korea, tripartite dialogue at the national level has facilitated the adoption of an all-embracing set of economic and social measures to cope with the Asian financial crisis. The measures have so far been successful in ensuring social stability.
- In South Africa, social dialogue has played a crucial role in ensuring a relatively smooth political and economic transition. Following several decades of apartheid and economic isolation, new democratic institutions have been successfully established. Major social and economic reforms have been adopted through a consensus-building process. Discussions at institutions such as the National Economic Development and Labour Council (NEDLAC) that gather together government, unions, employers and representatives of civil society, have been instrumental in this respect.
- The well-established tradition of social dialogue between the social partners in Switzerland lies at the heart of the country's economic and international success. Social peace is an important consideration when firms make

decisions about their location, particularly in the case of high value added activities that require large research and development investments and hence a stable, long-term planning horizon.

Several of the country studies have analysed the important role women have played in their country's economic development and in increasing its international competitiveness. For example, in Mauritius over the past 15 years, women have entered the labour market so rapidly that their share of total employment rose from 22 per cent to 33 per cent between 1982 and 1995. Similarly, in Bangladesh the majority of the workers employed in the rapidly expanding garment sector are women. It is important to note, however, that these and other countries still need to address the problem of a continuing degree of labour market inequality between men and women. In Mauritius, as elsewhere, women's rapidly increasing labour market qualifications (such as improved education levels and years of work experience) should lead to rapid commensurate improvements in women's labour market position, something which is not yet occurring.

Despite the neutral or positive links between the respect for core standards and the economic and social gains to be made from globalization, there remain many cases of non-enforcement. There are several reasons for this apparent paradox. Firstly, individual employers can increase their profits by denying their workers basic rights – even though this is an inefficient practice for the economy as a whole. Secondly, workers and their families are sometimes so poor that they have to accept jobs in which their basic rights are not respected; certain forms of child labour, for instance, may be difficult to eradicate owing to the extreme poverty of the children's families. Thirdly, the non-enforcement of certain standards, notably freedom of association rights, tends to go hand in hand with the non-enforcement of political and civil rights. Finally, some governments may be tempted to adopt low core standards in particular export sectors or export processing zones in the hope of stimulating exports or attracting foreign investment. More research is needed to address the relative importance of these different explanations behind the non-enforcement of core labour standards, bearing in mind that any solution to this controversial issue contributes to promoting the respect for the basic rights of workers, while at the same time promoting the economic prospects of all countries, notably developing ones.

CONCLUDING REMARKS

One clear outcome of this project has been the recognition of the importance of examining the interactions between globalization, economic development and social progress. All too often, these issues have been treated as separate phenomena, when they are increasingly interrelated. An integrated approach would no doubt yield a more realistic policy discussion. For instance, as discussed in this report, advocates of social progress should acknowledge the key role of trade and investment liberalization in creating new business opportunities and raising living standards. But trade specialists should also listen to the legitimate concerns and aspirations of vulnerable groups that may be affected by free-trade policies. Adopting freer trade and investment policies, while also ensuring that all individuals participate in the process on an equal footing (by way of the four social pillars identified in this report), should pave the way for a dynamic market economy that is socially sustainable.

It has to be said that, in practice, the task involves difficult trade-offs, at both national and international levels. For one thing, there is the issue of the sequence or the relative speed required between different reforms. Thus, many developing countries are finding it difficult to cope with the social consequences of the reduction in trade barriers predicted in WTO Agreements (e.g. in the case of the elimination of the Multifibre Arrangement or the budgetary problems caused by lower import tariffs). These countries need time to build the institutional infrastructures that will enable them to participate meaningfully in the world economy and make their voice heard. They should avoid being tempted to slow down efforts in the areas of basic education, social protection and basic workers' rights, with the aim of "improving international competitiveness" or "making room for lower taxes". Coordinated assistance from developed countries and international organizations, on both the trade and social fronts, would be welcomed.

The extent to which income inequalities can be addressed, while at the same time maintaining the incentives to innovate, invest and create jobs, is another complex issue. Globalization and the diffusion of ICT have paved the way for the advent of a "new economy". Inevitably, some will gain more than others from this process. This partly reflects the differences in individuals' abilities and in their willingness to take risks, which need to be rewarded. But many of those who do not participate in the "new economy" could become more productive if they had the appropriate training and technical means at their disposal. In this sense, governments need to think of ways of reducing the risk of a "digital divide".

The role of the tax system as a traditional redistribution mechanism is being eroded and is a matter of concern vis-à-vis certain ILO objectives. For a number of reasons, high-income groups have become increasingly mobile, and pressures to reduce tax rates on these groups have grown. The report shows that in most of the countries for which comparable data exist, the top marginal tax rates on individual incomes have been cut. This raises problems that can only be addressed at the international level, and which are important from the point of view of the financing of social protection and education systems.

Finally, the volatility of capital flows has a strong bearing on employment and social progress in ILO member States and, in future international debates on financial, trade and macroeconomic issues, the ILO could take a stronger role in ensuring that social and labour market dimensions are duly being taken into account.

SUMMARIES OF THE COUNTRY STUDIES

Bangladesh

One important issue in the international debate on globalization is whether there is a risk of developing countries becoming marginalized. There is some concern that the economic and social structures of these countries are too weak to sustain import liberalization, while their export prospects would allegedly be narrowly based.

The experience of Bangladesh is interesting in this respect. Per capita income is, on average, less than US$300 per year and one Bangladeshi inhabitant in four is officially estimated to be poor. Over 60 per cent of the population over the age of 15 is illiterate, while child labour is widespread despite the Government's commendable efforts: according to official statistics, over 6 million children are at work, that is, one child in five. Disturbingly, nearly 5 per cent of young children (aged 5 to 7) are reported to be working.

Against this background, the country embarked in the early 1990s on an ambitious process of trade liberalization, which has translated into an effective reduction of import tariffs, the abolition of many quotas and other non-tariff barriers, and the adoption of measures to promote exports and encourage foreign direct investment (FDI), notably through the creation of two export processing zones (EPZs). These measures are all the more impressive in that, until the early 1980s, import substitution was regarded as a key aspect of development strategy. The issue arises, therefore, as to whether this radical reorientation in economic policies may have contributed to improving the country's economic and social prospects.

The study shows that trade liberalization has gone hand in hand with positive developments in certain areas:

• During the 1990s, exports increased by a factor of four, thereby permitting a significant proportion of imports to be financed. Imports have also exhibited considerable dynamism; over the same period, GDP increased by about 4.5 per cent per year on average, much faster than population growth. This has contributed to improving real per capita income by one-fifth, on average. By contrast, during the 1970s and 1980s output grew modestly, thus explaining the stagnation of living standards during these years.

- A growth cycle has been set in motion, with rising real incomes making room for greater domestic savings and investment, which in turn provide healthy ground for future growth prospects. Thus, the investment effort has been gradually increased to 15–17 per cent of gross domestic product (GDP); reflecting the improved economic environment, between 4.5 and 5 million new jobs have been created (on a net basis) and the underemployment rate has declined (to some extent in the overall economy). Some real wage increases, broadly in line with productivity gains, have also been registered.

These results, modest as they are, have marked a departure from the previous situation of economic stagnation. Moreover, the political context of these achievements is one of a move away from martial law towards the restoration in the 1980s of a multi-party democratic system.

Unfortunately, however, trade liberalization and the associated growth process have also been accompanied by increased inequalities. It is estimated that the average real income of the 20 per cent poorest households has practically stagnated since 1989–90, while the living standards of the 20 per cent richest households have leapt forward – the average per capita income of these households having increased by over 30 per cent. This may explain why both poverty rates and the incidence of child labour have not been reduced much. Development has also been unequal between urban and rural areas. Pockets of development around the capital and the two EPZs have enjoyed a dynamic economic environment compared with the rest of the country. According to a conceptual framework developed for the purposes of the study, the trend towards greater inequality may have been caused by the fact that the stimulatory effects associated with trade liberalization have operated in the context of a "dual" economy, one where rural and urban sectors follow independent development paths.

There is also apprehension over job losses in the import-competing manufacturing sector. In the same context, some industries are finding it difficult to withstand increased imports of low-priced or dumped products, arising from smuggling with border areas of India. Furthermore, privatization has led to large-scale retrenchment of workers, while according to some findings few efficiency gains have been realized. Indeed, the change in ownership has generally not been accompanied by improved management of privatized enterprises.

Social conflicts in the form of nationwide "political" strikes (the so-called *hartals*) have tended to intensify of late. These might have sent a wrong signal to the much-needed foreign investments in general and in the energy sector in particular, where bright prospects exist for exploiting the country's rich gas reserves.

Finally, the country's low per capita income, accompanied by a concentration of exports on a few low value added products, insufficient flows of foreign direct investment and proneness to natural disasters, all point to its vulnerability in the global environment of trade liberalization and increasing competition, and are indicative of the major challenges ahead.

Addressing these problems is probably the most difficult task for policy-makers and the social partners. Wider participation of the population in the gains from globalization would be justified from both the social and economic points of view. This study, therefore, examines possible areas for policy action. First, there is an obvious need to improve access to education. However, it is also important to note that primary education receives little attention compared with university education – often reserved for an elite. It is illustrative that, on average, the State spends yearly the equivalent of US\$14 per pupil in primary schools, compared with over US\$500 per university student. The teaching time in many primary schools is only two hours per day. Secondly, bureaucratic hurdles are sometimes an impediment to FDI, thereby reducing the ability of the country to exploit its export capacity. Thirdly, encouraging collective bargaining in public and private enterprises would help reduce tensions at the national level, where wages are often set. The elimination of the ban of unions in EPZs would help reduce social conflicts while allowing a more consensus-based, participatory climate. Fourthly, the study identifies other measures in banking reform and export promotion that could contribute to enhancing the gains from globalization. Fifthly, the revival of economic growth recorded in the 1990s should help strengthen social safety net programmes as part of the Government's national policy of alleviating poverty and providing training programmes for retrenched workers.

In sum, the country is going through the initial stages of the economic take-off. In order to accelerate the pace of development, it is important that the Government and the social partners undertake a range of social and economic reforms with a view to distributing the gains from globalization more evenly. The Grameen Bank as well as other initiatives of non-governmental organizations (NGOs), replicated in many countries, indicate that there is potential for solving these problems, including some of the most thorny ones such as poverty alleviation.

Chile

Chile is a remarkable example of a country that has integrated well into the world economy. Before trade liberalization was initiated in the early 1970s, import tariffs exceeded 90 per cent, on average, and non-tariff barriers were pervasive. Following a short period of trade restrictions, trade liberalization has been gathering momentum again since the mid-1980s. Today, Chile's trade regime is one of the most liberal in the world, for which the Chilean Government recently won praise from the World Trade Organization (WTO). Reflecting the liberalization process, trade and investment flows have been growing rapidly, both in dollar terms and as a share of gross domestic product (GDP).

During its relatively long initial phase, trade liberalization in Chile was accompanied by economic and social costs of some size. Since the mid-1980s, however, GDP has grown uninterruptedly at a healthy rate of 7 per cent, on average, and inflation has been brought down to single-digit levels. In addition, the country has no fiscal deficit. The relatively large current account deficit is the result of private-sector savings/investment imbalances, which are officially estimated to be sustainable. These favourable macroeconomic conditions are reflected in the employment figures: since the mid-1980s, over 1.5 million jobs have been created, thereby reducing the unemployment rate, which, at the end of the 1990s, stood at less than 6 per cent. During the same period, poverty has halved to one-quarter of the population and health indicators also show substantial improvements.

These results compare favourably with other countries in Latin America and elsewhere. They clearly demonstrate the benefits to be gained from trade liberalization, which, in the eyes of many observers, has transformed Chile into a "model" of economic reform.

Social progress, however, has been uneven. Firstly, income distribution is relatively unequal by international standards, with the richest population quintile earning 57 per cent of the national income and the poorest quintile a mere 4 per cent. Trends in the late 1990s, moreover, pointed to widening inequalities. Secondly, and perhaps more importantly, the distribution of opportunities is also unequal. In practice, the educational system is divided by social origin, and there is a clear difference between private schools, many of which are of excellent quality but extremely expensive, and public schools, which are of substantially lower quality. Less than one-third of the children of relatively poorly educated fathers complete secondary education, while the proportion is over 90 per cent for children growing up in more educated households. Although improvements have recently been made in the public system, a large gap remains in the quality of public and private schools. Thirdly, a relatively large number of the jobs being created include little or no employment or social protection, and the situation appears to be worsening. Less than two-thirds of Chilean salaried workers, for example, have a written employment contract, with adequate coverage for social protection.

It has been claimed that the statistics that are available exaggerate the gravity of these social and labour problems. Though there is probably an element of truth in this claim, observations and anecdotal evidence suggest that, however imperfect they may be, statistics do reflect reality.

Several factors, which are more or less directly related to the globalization process, account for these social and labour problems:

- Chilean exports concentrate heavily on natural resources and processed natural resources with low value added. This type of specialization makes the country prone to a high degree of income inequality, since the owners of these natural resources tend to be few in number and are likely to belong to relatively wealthy sectors of the population. Econometric estimates suggest that trade has contributed to income and wage inequalities, although the impact appears to be small.
- Many new jobs have been created in resource extraction (agriculture, including fishing and forestry, and mining), where most employment is characterized by instability and/or substantial health hazards (a high risk of accidents or an extensive use of pesticides). Although high-quality jobs have also been created in export-oriented sectors, especially in the area of resource processing, their numbers seem comparably low.
- The prices of Chile's main export products are extremely volatile, and this creates an element of instability in production and employment levels. This, in turn, might explain the prevalence of a relatively large proportion of unstable jobs, as well as the high rate of labour turnover.
- There is some evidence that technological change is skill based, to the detriment of the wages and working conditions of unskilled workers, who tend to be concentrated in poorer segments of the population.
- As in many countries, the productive system is undergoing profound change. In Chile, enterprises are increasingly resorting to outsourcing and subcontracting practices, which also entail a measure of labour market instability.
- Collective bargaining institutions are relatively weak in Chile, making it difficult for low-wage workers to bargain for better working conditions (skilled workers are typically more mobile, which consequently reinforces their bargaining position).

So should measures be taken to address these problems while at the same time maintaining the dynamism of Chile's economy? Some would claim that, to the extent that the Chilean economy continues to enjoy high growth rates, income distribution will gradually become slightly less unequal as more stable jobs are created. It could also be argued that these labour and social problems have little bearing on economic performance. However, both these arguments can be challenged. Despite proven government expertise in the area of macroeconomic policy management, the Chilean economy is not immune to shocks – in fact its comparative advantage in natural-resource-based goods makes Chile's economy vulnerable to changes in terms of trade. The recent financial crisis in Asia, which is an important market for Chilean exports, has affected the country's economic prospects and threatens to trigger a substantial increase in the unemployment rate. Given the relatively poor social protection of many workers, this downturn could have dramatic implications for large segments of the population. Moreover, there is a complex relationship at work between inequalities and instability, on the one hand, and international specialization and economic performance, on the other. For example, it is difficult to improve productivity when job security is low, which, in turn, reduces the economy's potential for growth. Even though individuals at the low end of the income spectrum have an incentive to improve human capital (the incentive being all the greater, the wider the income gap), there are obvious practical obstacles to this upgrading process materializing. On the other hand, in a situation of low productivity, the Chilean economy will continue to specialize in sectors characterized by unstable jobs, which contribute to income inequalities. These factors may result in a low-productivity, unstable jobs' trap.

The study explores several policy avenues open to Chile if it is to avoid this trap while maintaining its economy on a healthy footing, not only in education, but also in social protection, labour regulations, the build-up of training institutions at the sectoral level, and research and development (R&D) incentives, as well as social dialogue at the national level, which was still rather limited at the end of the 1990s. Some of these measures have budgetary costs, involving difficult trade-offs between short-term objectives, such as maintaining a constant tax rate, and long-term ones, for example, participating in a globalizing economy in a way that is socially sustainable.

In short, the Chilean experience shows that trade liberalization can stimulate job creation and at the same time raise national income levels. However, in Chile it is doing little to correct (and it may even be aggravating) the country's high levels of social inequality and labour market instability. This suggests that the link between trade liberalization and social progress is neither automatic nor problem-free. Policies need to address this problem, otherwise Chile may find itself trapped in low productivity, which will ultimately jeopardize the country's social stability.

Republic of Korea

Until the end of 1997, the Republic of Korea (henceforth Korea) was widely regarded as one of the most spectacular success stories of modern capitalism. In the late 1950s, it emerged from the ashes of a civil war as one of the poorest countries in the world, with an income per capita of less than US$100 per year. But then the economy started to expand rapidly, allowing for an impressive improvement in living standards and the creation of over 10 million jobs. During the 1980s and 1990s, the unemployment rate remained at a low 2–3 per cent, and women's labour force participation rate rose steadily. Furthermore, judging from the sound fiscal position of government accounts and the continuing improvement of income distribution, the situation looked sustainable, so that most observers, including international investors, were optimistic about the country's economic prospects. Then came the Asian financial crisis of November 1997, and the spectacular period of development came to a sudden and unexpected halt.

Until the crisis, the main driving force behind Korea's outstanding economic performance had been the country's government-led, export-oriented growth strategy. Between 1970 and the late 1990s, the volume of trade multiplied by a factor of five (in real terms). The ratio of trade to gross domestic product (GDP) soared from below 20 per cent in the 1960s to over 60 per cent in the early 1980s and has broadly stabilized since then. Importantly, Korea's presence in world markets has risen substantially: Korean exports represent a noticeable 2.5 per cent of world exports, compared with an almost negligible figure in the early 1960s, and it is estimated that about 3.5 million people work, directly or indirectly, in the export sector. These developments have gone hand in hand with profound structural changes in trade patterns, with Korea emerging as an important exporter of relatively technologically advanced products. Government-intensified research and development (R&D) investment has helped improve the technological capacity of the country, constituting a major asset in an era of globalization.

Likewise, foreign direct investment (FDI) has instilled dynamism into the Korean economy. Interestingly, direct investment inflows have tended to create relatively skill-intensive jobs, whereas FDI outflows have been concentrated in unskilled labour-intensive sectors. On average, foreign companies in Korea pay higher wages and offer better working conditions than domestic firms.

Besides trade, the impressive improvement in Korea's education system explains much of the country's growth. Education has traditionally been a major priority in Korea. Access to secondary education was made available to everyone in the 1960s and early 1970s and, since then, substantial efforts have been made to improve tertiary education. Thus, in 1995, nearly 60 per cent of young people were enrolled in tertiary education, compared with only 9 per cent in 1970, and one-fifth of the Korean population over the age of 25 has a college degree. As a result of these efforts, Korea has surpassed several developed countries in educational attainment levels. This study shows that improvements in education have contributed to alleviating the pressures towards labour market inequalities that can be associated with globalization. Technological change stands out as an important source of inequality, while trade has played a relatively minor role and education has mitigated both factors.

However, certain aspects of the globalization process have proved to be unsustainable in Korea:

- The ability of sizeable stocks of financial capital to move across countries almost instantaneously.
- A corporate governance system characterized by a lack of transparency in management responsibilities, close ties between industry and banks, and relatively weak internal competition.
- A proneness to finance development through debt. With the rapid intensification of financial market globalization, industries have funded their long-term investment plans through short-term external debt, creating an unsustainable financial situation. More generally, the liberalization of short-term capital flows, at a time when Korean financial markets were still weak, has proved problematic.
- The denial of basic labour rights, in particular until the declaration of democracy in 1987. The increasingly tight labour market conditions should have helped exert pressure to increase wages in line with productivity gains, thereby providing an incentive for selecting investment projects more cautiously. This process, however, has been delayed. In addition, repressed labour rights have created a confrontational situation in many enterprises.

Towards the end of 1997, foreign banks, reflecting a loss of confidence in Korea, refused to renew credit lines to their Korean counterparts. Rather than default on its debt obligations, the Government discussed a rescue package with the International Monetary Fund (IMF). Worth about US$56 billion, this package includes stabilization and structural adjustment conditions in the areas of industrial restructuring, bank reform, social security and the labour market, with the aim of sharing the burden of adjustment as fairly as possible. However, the corporate governance reform is taking longer than expected, while the process of laying off workers has resumed and is gathering momentum. FDI in

Korea has so far been relatively modest, depriving the country of much-needed stable, long-term injections of capital.

The study also examines the policy issues that arise when the prime objective is to speed up the adjustment process in the face of a crisis, and all the while making the globalization process socially sustainable:

- A well-functioning training system is a key factor behind international competitiveness. Since the start of the crisis, the Government has put more emphasis on training the unemployed. The system has to take into consideration two major problems, namely the relevance of training to labour market requirements and the risk of free-riding, which arises when workers trained by one enterprise are "poached" by another firm. Several countries (including Germany and, more recently, Argentina) have succeeded in addressing this problem by organizing training at the sectoral or industry level with the participation of the social partners, and by sharing training costs and benefits with all the interested parties.

- Substantial reforms of the labour law have been announced. One aim is to provide a legal basis for dismissals on economic grounds. It is important to recognize that, in cases such as bankruptcies, lay-offs are often unavoidable, and creating obstacles to dismissals can aggravate matters. However, the process has to take certain factors into consideration. In particular, some categories of the labour force (women and older workers, for example) tend to be discriminated against when lay-offs are being considered, and so they need to be protected. In addition, an effective severance payment needs to be ensured; the recent setting up of the Wage Claim Guarantee Fund is an important step in this direction.

- Korea's social safety net has long rested on individual enterprises. For example, in the case of pensions, firms contribute to the Retirement Allowances System. However, when contributions are not transferred to the fund, in times of difficulty, workers losing their jobs also risk losing the part of their pension rights not covered by the Wage Claim Guarantee Fund, as well as other benefits. This state of affairs would very likely add to workers' resistance in the face of lay-offs.

- Many firms currently in financial difficulties might, however, have good long-term prospects. In such cases, a temporary subsidy to help maintain employment levels would be useful. In the countries where such temporary subsidies exist and are well administered, it has been shown that it is crucial that the subsidies: (a) are of limited duration (usually not longer than six months); (b) do not fully compensate for the loss of wages due to shorter working hours; and (c) are closely monitored by local labour offices. Provided these conditions are met, temporary employment subsidies can be a cost-effective way of easing the social cost of a crisis. It can also limit the loss of human capital associated with lay-offs.

- In several countries, unemployment benefits are not entirely cut off when the unemployed person accepts a low-paid job, the intention being to avoid the so-called "unemployment trap".
- Recent legal changes regarding freedom of association and the right to collective bargaining should improve industrial relations. The workers will then have to choose between the relative merits and demerits of a bargaining system based on either a single workers' representation (designated by way of free, democratic elections in the enterprise) or a multiple union system. According to some, the latter runs the risk of fragmenting the workers' voice, while generating inefficiency; under this system, the employer has to negotiate with every single workers' organization.

Finally, it can be safely asserted that, in the wake of Korea's financial crisis, the creation of a national tripartite committee has been instrumental in formulating a consistent policy framework. International experience suggests that such frameworks can help create consensus on the most urgent issues, and at the same time pave the way for growth based on a socially sustainable and open economic system.

Mauritius

It is generally accepted that Mauritius has been a success story in the past decade and a half – the country has even been referred to as an African miracle. Since the balance-of-payments crisis of the early 1980s, real national income has risen by an average of nearly 6 per cent per year and real gross domestic product (GDP) per capita by around 4 per cent per year. Just as impressive, this rapid and sustained economic growth has not been associated with some of the negative aspects of globalization and development experienced by other countries. Evidence suggests that income distribution has improved, while socio-economic benefits such as education, health services and housing amenities now reach virtually everyone. Importantly, Mauritius has a functioning democracy; tripartism, though not fully developed, plays an important role in the country's policy-making.

There is little doubt that international trade and global markets have played an important role in Mauritius' recent success. Many new jobs, for example, have been created in the export sectors, especially in the garment industry, with the result that the unemployment rate dropped sharply in the 1980s; between 1982 and 1988, new jobs in trade-related sectors represented approximately 20 per cent of the country's total employment.

Mauritius' success appears to be due, in large part, to the following conditions:

- The country's good social and political climate, which has enabled Mauritius to attract foreign direct investment (FDI) and to take advantage of its outward-looking development strategies. Social stability owes much to the existence of a social safety net and, more generally, to the widespread belief that all segments of the population can gain something from international trade.
- The preferential access of its main export products, such as garments, to the European Union (EU) under the Lomé Convention, and sugar, again through a special agreement with the EU. Exports have also been promoted by the Government through an export processing zone (EPZ), which enjoys special tax and financial privileges, although this is now under government review.
- Since the 1980s, the export sector has had the advantage of: (a) a semi-skilled labour force and high literacy rates; and (b) the availability of an underused female labour force, especially in the garment sector.
- The gradual liberalization of import barriers, which smoothed the adjustment of domestic-oriented enterprises to import competition, while continuing to provide substantial government revenues.
- The existence of a high savings rate and the rapid increase in the participation rate of women in the labour force.

Mauritius has now reached a crossroads in its development. Not only is it expected to lose its preferential trade benefits in the near future, but it is also finding it increasingly difficult to compete with newly emerging low-wage garment-producing countries specializing in low-skilled manufacture, as shown in recent years by the relocation of the manufacture of these products to Madagascar. FDI in the EPZ has also fallen recently.

Strains in the labour market linked to international trade patterns have begun to show. Unemployment rose in the 1990s, due, in part, to poor employment growth in Mauritius' main export sectors; indeed, employment levels in the sugar and garment/textile sectors fell substantially in the 1990s.

There are also fiscal strains: the government tax base has been eroded by the reduced tariff rates accompanying trade liberalization (previously taxes on international trade made up the largest share of government revenue).

So what can be done to address these challenges? The Government has emphasized the need to increase productivity in the face of globalization, and has envisaged four outward-looking "cylinders of growth": sugar, garments/textiles, tourism and skilled labour-intensive services such as international banking. Government objectives are to: (a) move upmarket in sugar and garment exports by investing and upgrading the skills of the country's labour force; (b) improve Mauritius' position as a high-quality tourist destination; and (c) develop a financial and high-technology centre for southern Africa (similar, it is hoped, to Singapore's position in Asia). In order to understand the problems that may arise from this high-productivity strategy, it is useful to bear in mind several considerations:

- It is important to maintain social stability, which is a major factor underlying Mauritius' successful international integration so far, and which implies maintaining the country's welfare state.
- It will be necessary to compensate for stagnant revenues brought about by the reduction of import tariffs by increasing tax revenues from other sources and/or altering spending. Whichever methods are used, tax revenues need to maintain their progressive nature, while changing spending means examining Mauritius' present distribution of social expenditure, which is characterized by a relatively high share (by international standards) going to pensions.
- The skill level of the labour force needs to be improved. This will include increasing the number of highly skilled people, if Mauritius is to develop into a high-tech and financial centre. Only 2.5 per cent of Mauritius' labour force has a university degree at present, which is low when compared with other countries that specialize in skilled labour activities. This also means improving the general quality of education, and in particular reducing the high failure rate of the Certificate of Primary Education (CPE) exam.
- At present the Government provides financial incentives to certain sectors and not to others. Since it is always difficult to pick the "right" sector, it might be worth creating more of a level playing field, where all small and medium-sized enterprises (SMEs) and large businesses in the EPZ have the same tax and credit incentives. Backward linkages between large export enterprises and SMEs also need more encouragement, even though this is difficult in a small economy.
- Labour laws and regulations based on tripartite consensus need to be regularly updated. In an era of globalization, where it pays to be adaptable, greater reliance on collective bargaining and less reliance on government intervention in the labour market are recommended.
- More gender-sensitive policies need to be considered. By taking into account women's improved levels of education and their commitment to the labour market, Mauritius could increase its labour market efficiency and international competitiveness.

• In view of the difficult policy challenges arising from globalization, there is a need to increase the amount of labour market information available by, for example, conducting more frequent labour force surveys.

These policy challenges are difficult. Moreover, decisions will have to be taken in a climate characterized by a certain degree of anxiety. Mauritius, though, does have certain advantages, such as its stable political system, good physical infrastructure, the existence of tripartite institutions, a high savings rate and a relatively well-trained, semi-skilled labour force. The process of regional integration, in particular in the Southern Africa Development Community (SADC) region, might help to diversify export markets, while also supporting the upgrading of production. Mauritius needs to take advantage of its current high economic growth to address these issues immediately, since the foreseeable loss of its preferential trade arrangements and the more challenging international economic environment of the near future will make carrying out these policies more difficult.

In a recent joint paper submitted to the World Trade Organization (WTO), the Government of Mauritius, together with five other small countries, asked that trade liberalization and trade preferences take into account the vulnerability of small economies, which are felt to be at a disadvantage in today's globalized economy. Distance from the main markets, vulnerability to large price shocks for often important export commodities and reliance on a small number of export products (because their economies are too small to develop economies of scale) were some of the factors cited in the paper. Fiji and Mauritius have submitted additional case study papers to the WTO.

In the meantime, the country may face a difficult transition period. Unemployment is rising, since, as noted in this report, employment creation in the designated four cylinders of growth is not enough to absorb the expected increase in the labour force. Mauritius needs to pay special attention to vulnerable and disadvantaged groups during this period. Furthermore, the social partners need to be closely involved in social and economic policies and in decision-making. Finally, it is important that Mauritius, a self-confessed welfare State, does not succumb to the "conventional wisdom" of some neoclassical economists, who wish to see the welfare State dismantled and social services privatized.

Poland

Poland used to be regarded as a country with difficult, indeed almost insurmountable, economic problems. At the end of the 1980s, following several decades of central planning strategies, the country faced the challenge of adapting its structures and institutions to market principles. The task was further complicated by the country's large external debt, the servicing of which absorbed a significant part of available hard currency receipts. In the face of these difficulties, the then Government adopted an all-embracing programme of reforms, which initiated a period of economic and social transition, encompassing, inter alia, price deregulation, privatization and trade liberalization.

Developments during the first stages of the transition process were marked by rapidly falling output and employment levels, and most forecasts predicted a further deterioration in the economic climate. Since then, however, the performance of the Polish economy has been impressive. Since 1993, growth in gross domestic product (GDP) has averaged 5.5 per cent, while the unemployment rate has dropped to between 10.5 and 11 per cent, down by more than 4 percentage points from its 1993 peak. The liberalization of international trade has proceeded at a relatively fast pace. Many non-tariff barriers have been dismantled and the average import tariff rate has been reduced to a mere 3.3 per cent. Foreign direct investment (FDI) flows have also been liberalized. The volume of foreign trade has more than trebled, with the European Union (EU) becoming the main trading partner, and Poland has become an important location of multinational affiliates. More fundamentally, the private sector has become the main engine of the economy, currently representing nearly 70 per cent of national output and employment.

The speed and depth of the transition process make it difficult to isolate the specific impact of globalization vis-à-vis other factors such as privatization. Within these strict limitations, this study suggests that trade and FDI have indeed contributed to the economic expansion recorded since the early 1990s. Despite the "downsizing" effects often associated with the restructuring process in general and trade liberalization in particular, Poland has tended to specialize in the export of labour-intensive products. In addition, there is some evidence that FDI has contributed to expanding the production and export capacities of the country; average wages in foreign-owned manufacturing companies are 50 per cent higher than in the domestic manufacturing private sector. It can be safely claimed that trade and investment liberalization has contributed to upgrading and modernizing the production system.

Economic and socio-political factors seem to suggest that these positive trends could continue. Firstly, there is still a considerable amount of unused capacity, which could make room for further increases in output and living standards; in particular, a large proportion of the labour force is either unemployed or underemployed. Thus, agriculture comprises over one-quarter of total employment but only 6 per cent of GDP. Secondly, the country is involved in negotiations for its accession to the EU, which, combined with the pursuit of reforms in several areas, should continue to stimulate FDI inflows and trade. Thirdly, the historical ties between the workers' movement and the Government have facilitated the transition process, making it socially acceptable.

Important as they are, these factors should not divert attention from the fact that the process of growth in Poland is unbalanced, which is not only problematic from the social point of view but also for reasons of economic efficiency:

- The Polish economy has strong regional disparities. It appears that the gains from globalization have been limited to the capital, Warsaw, and to a few urban centres. Warsaw alone has attracted over two-fifths of the total FDI inflows, and empirical evidence shown in this study suggests that it is also the main beneficiary of the country's impressive export record. Between 1992 and 1997, reflecting the regional concentration of trade and FDI, employment in Warsaw increased by almost 30 per cent, while at the same time 15 of Poland's 49 provinces or voivodships suffered net employment losses. Therefore, a situation of near full employment has developed in the large cities: in 1998 unemployment was between 2.5 and 4 per cent. By contrast, unemployment remains high in most other parts of the country: in 1998, two voivodships still had unemployment rates in excess of 20 per cent.
- Regional disparities have had a strong bearing on macroeconomic developments. Indeed, reflecting the tight labour market conditions, wages have grown rapidly in the major urban centres, particularly in Warsaw. Despite the nominal depreciation of the Polish currency, the zloty, this has led to an erosion of the cost-competitiveness of Polish exports. Reflecting these trends, the current account deficit has deteriorated significantly and, although the deficit is largely financed by stable capital inflows, it may be difficult to sustain such a situation over the medium term.

It is sometimes claimed that market forces progressively contribute to redressing these imbalances. There is certainly an incentive for: (a) investors (domestic and foreign) to locate production in rural areas where costs are relatively low; (b) low-income agricultural workers to move to economically dynamic urban centres; and (c) outward-looking enterprises, notably in the agro-food industry, to create "backward linkages" with suppliers in the countryside. In practice, however, these incentives are often too weak (or they operate too slowly). This is because the regional imbalances in Poland are mainly attributable to structural factors, most of which can only be corrected by government intervention, in cooperation with the social partners. Firstly, internal migration flows have been constrained by the high rents and housing prices in the main urban centres, and many households in rural areas regard agricultural land as a safety net, for historical as well as socio-cultural reasons. Secondly, except in Warsaw and the country's other large cities, the physical infrastructure network is notoriously inadequate, thereby reducing the trade and development potential of both the rural economy and the country as a whole. Roads, railways, telecommunications and, particularly, motorways increasingly cannot sustain the rapid phase of expansion. Thirdly, the vocational training system has been slow to adapt, sometimes generating a mismatch between the skills acquired at school and labour market requirements. The problem has been especially acute in rural areas. Fourthly, institutional support for the diversification of the agricultural sector is still relatively weak.

This study examines these policy issues in some depth and documents recent government initiatives that should help address these problems. It considers the development of physical infrastructure and human capital as a relatively urgent policy priority. Action in this area would no doubt improve Poland's chances of successfully integrating into the EU. At the same time, the Government plans substantial cuts in corporate and personal income taxes – both of which would then bring them to levels significantly lower than in most EU countries. There is a danger that, in the absence of efforts to tackle the regional imbalances, lower taxes will actually aggravate them. Therefore, in view of the much-needed improvements in infrastructure and education, it might be useful to consider implementing a tax reform over a longer time span than is presently planned. This is a difficult trade-off, and one that deserves extensive dialogue within the framework of national tripartite institutions.

South Africa

The past few years have been a historical turning point in South African political and economic systems. In 1994, following several decades of apartheid, democratic elections were held and new institutions comprising representatives from all the major social groups emerged. The new Government initiated a much-needed process of economic reform, aimed at creating an outward-looking economy. This went hand in hand with efforts to improve social equity and income distribution.

At the start of the transformation process, the challenge facing South Africa was widely regarded as immense (and the risk of political instability was considered to be high). Several decades of relative economic isolation meant that firms were ill prepared to take advantage of the opportunities arising from trade liberalization, while the potential adjustment costs were correspondingly high. A major recession during the early 1990s led to falling living standards for the majority of the population. In addition, previous economic policies had tended to favour capital-intensive sectors, to the detriment of labour-intensive ones – a rather strange policy considering the country has such an abundant, but unused, labour force. In 1994, the unemployment rate reached alarmingly high levels. More fundamentally, following several decades of segregation, the African population was hoping for a rapid improvement in political rights, as well as better social and economic conditions. The main policy issue was, therefore, to satisfy these legitimate aspirations and at the same time create a stable macroeconomic framework to enhance the integration of South Africa into the international economy. Objectively, however, the initial economic conditions made the task problematic: the country was simply not prepared to take advantage of economic and trade reforms.

Today, it is clear that the country's economic performance has exceeded expectations. Economic growth has recovered slightly (from 1994 to 1998, GDP growth rose by a modest annual average of 2.7 per cent), inflation is on a downward trend and there are no major fiscal or financial imbalances. Trade liberalization has got under way, including a scheduled gradual decrease in import tariffs in force since 1994, allowing for a significant increase in trade flows. Not only have most non-tariff barriers been lifted, but tariff rates have also been brought down and are expected to be reduced further over the next few years. Export subsidies have been suppressed. South Africa has become an active member of the World Trade Organization (WTO), it is the most important member of the Southern African Development Community (SADC) and is engaged in trade discussions with the European Union (EU). Likewise, progress has been made in the area of foreign direct investment (FDI) liberalization. At least until the November 1997 Asian crisis, FDI inflows were on the rise.

The situation on the employment front, however, has deteriorated. Unemployment remains high and has been increasing, endangering social stability and contributing to the rise in the crime rate. Some have argued that trade and FDI liberalization have substantially aggravated the employment situation, presumably because higher imports would have caused job losses. The study examines this issue closely and comes to the following conclusions:

- Since the start of trade liberalization, employment has been falling at a slower rate.
- Surprisingly, relative employment losses in manufacturing import-competing sectors taken as a whole have been less important than in export-oriented manufacturing sectors.
- The study provides theoretical support and empirical evidence that trade liberalization may have shifted production in favour of capital-intensive sectors to the detriment of labour-intensive ones. This finding reflects the

fact that South Africa specializes in capital-intensive products, which, according to several authors, is a legacy of past industrial policies. Further research remains to be done as to why trade liberalization and changes in industrial policies have not caused a shift to a more labour-intensive development path.

- Empirical analysis carried out in the study suggests that employment losses are not directly associated with greater import competition. Instead, they seem to be caused by a process of production rationalization (or "rightsizing"), which affects export-oriented sectors in particular. A key issue that needs to be resolved is to find out to what extent this process is associated with the necessity to become internationally competitive.

- Empirical evidence suggests that an increase in investment is associated with higher employment levels. In other words, an insufficient stock of physical capital may lie at the heart of the unemployment problem. It is important to note that investment in South Africa represents only about 17 per cent of GDP, which is low when compared with middle-income countries that have been successful in creating employment (in these countries, investment typically exceeds one-quarter of GDP).

- The South African economy suffers from a chronic shortage of skilled labour. This has negative consequences in terms of economic growth and may have hindered the development of labour-intensive sectors. In addition, it hampers the ability of the labour market to adapt to the instability often associated with globalization.

In short, the legacy of protective industrial policies that favoured capital-intensive sectors, together with a shortage of real and human capital, has reduced the ability of the South African economy to benefit from trade and FDI liberalization. The Government and the social partners have taken important steps to address the underlying factors at work:

- Measures to create a more competitive product-market environment have been announced – international experience suggests that removing obstacles to making the creation of small businesses easier would help maximize the benefits from trade and at the same time stimulate job creation.

- Education has become a major government priority. The principal aims are to improve its quality and raise school attendance levels.

- Labour regulations have been reformed to increase the adaptability of the labour market, while also providing a measure of employment security. Compared with other middle-income countries, labour regulations on dismissals, fixed-term contracts and working conditions do not appear to be particularly onerous for employers, which thus dismisses the view that inflexible labour markets are at the heart of the employment problem.

- Importantly, contained in all these measures is the explicit aim to promote the rights and working conditions of the African majority.

Despite these measures, the social situation in South Africa remains bleak. Further reforms, particularly in the field of creating a more favourable environment for business start-ups, may be needed. In addition, it will be important to assist disadvantaged groups in a way that does not reduce incentives to work, invest or to take initiative. In this regard, South Africa can draw on the extensive experience of targeted active labour market policies and social benefits worldwide.

While much remains to be done, social dialogue within the framework of the National Economic Development and Labour Council (NEDLAC) and other relevant institutions appears to be an important asset and one that can contribute to maintaining the momentum of reform in a consensual and socially sustainable way.

Switzerland

In many respects, Switzerland would seem to be one of the main beneficiaries from globalization. Despite its relatively small size, it is home to some of the world's most important multinational enterprises (MNEs). It is the 18th main exporter of goods in the world and the 13th in the export of services. Swiss enterprises have a solid reputation as reliable producers of innovative, high-quality products. This excellent performance is reflected in the country's enviable social indicators: all children, for instance, have access to high-quality public education; in 1996, the average annual income of Swiss nationals came close to US$25,000, while the unemployment rate has long been one of the lowest in Europe.

To some extent, these achievements can be attributed to the outward orientation of the Swiss economy. In particular, this study identifies three interrelated aspects of the Swiss "export model":

- There is evidence that Swiss exporters have specialized in niche markets that are characterized by a high degree of product differentiation. As a result, most of these exporters compete mainly in terms of product quality and innovation, rather than in terms of price. More fundamentally, recent theoretical developments confirmed by empirical research presented in this study show that this type of specialization can help attenuate the inequality pressures often associated with globalization. Indeed, it may be one reason why, in Switzerland, income inequality and precarious employment have not increased as much as in other countries.

- A skilled labour force is a crucial element of this niche-type strategy, and a solid educational system is a key feature. Perhaps more importantly, a well-developed vocational training system helps workers adapt their skills to ever-changing economic conditions.
- Consensus-based industrial relations have been instrumental in preserving social stability, which is especially important for encouraging long-term investments and for activities that have a high research and development (R&D) intensity, such as the pharmaceutical, machinery and engineering industries, as well as specialized financial services.

These are important assets in the era of globalization. Switzerland, however, has not exploited all the gains that would have been expected of the country, as can be seen from its relatively poor employment and export record of the 1990s.

Since 1990–91, most economic and social indicators have deteriorated, not only vis-à-vis national, historical standards but also by international comparison. Low-skilled and older workers are finding themselves more vulnerable to job displacement and are facing difficulties in re-entering the labour market. The share of Swiss exports in the world total has declined substantially. Although far from alarming, this situation raises the issue of how the strengths of the Swiss economic system can be maintained, while addressing concerns about its relative stagnation. A combination of macroeconomic and structural factors may have contributed to this relatively disappointing performance.

Firstly, during most of the 1990s the Swiss economy operated under rather tight monetary conditions. High interest rates and large inflows of short-term capital were accompanied by a spectacular real appreciation of the currency. Since 1995 a relatively less stringent monetary policy has been pursued, given the extremely low rate of inflation, in a bid to facilitate economic growth. In addition, fiscal policy was tightened in the mid-1990s, thereby adding downward pressure on domestic demand.

Secondly, at a more structural level, competition in internal markets is relatively weak. Access to certain professions (such as medicine, the law and private professional services) is heavily regulated. Cartels are not uncommon but are considered unlawful if they significantly affect competition without justification on the grounds of economic efficiency, or if they lead to the suppression of effective competition. As in European Union (EU) law, the abuse of a dominant position is reprehensible and can justify legal action. New legislation has been introduced within the framework of an important reform programme in this field. Although it is too early to assess its results, it would appear that the process has been slow in certain cases, which may be one of the main reasons for the exceedingly high prices in Switzerland, which, according to evidence presented in this study, is the most expensive country in the world. High prices may also explain the wide gap between labour costs for the employers ("too high") and the purchasing power of wages for Swiss workers ("too low"). Indeed, this report confirms that Swiss wages are among the highest in the world (although unit labour costs need not be, since productivity is also high) but that, because of the high level of domestic prices, the real purchasing power of Swiss wages comes close to the average for developed countries. Domestic competition is also weak, inhibiting business initiatives and thereby reducing the country's potential for job creation.

Importantly, improving domestic competition would be justified not only from the point of view of economic efficiency but also for social reasons: high-income groups are the main beneficiaries of regulations that have the effect of restricting competition. Therefore, more competition in this area would improve income distribution and at the same time stimulate job creation. However, experience has shown that the opening up of certain sheltered sectors to competition tends to be accompanied by restructuring, with a consequential loss of jobs, which needs to be taken into account when the timetable for implementing liberalization policies is being decided. In the event of labour displacement, support measures would be needed.

This study examines the above issues as well as other policy requirements, particularly in the areas of training, labour regulations and social protection. The main finding is that, in comparison with other countries, Switzerland's labour regulatory framework provides for a relatively high degree of adaptability. This, however, does not appear to cause an unduly large amount of employment insecurity, except for the growing practice of having "on-call" workers in certain industries. The legal protection of these workers is limited and the social partners (employers' and workers' organizations) may need to consider ways of addressing this problem. More generally, the number of workers in low-paid jobs would seem to be on the rise. Improving their social protection, better targeting their training and introducing active labour market policies to meet their specific needs would be justified. Obviously, social dialogue is of paramount importance for addressing the problems faced by workers, especially those who are badly paid and low skilled.

Fears regarding wages and employment have been exacerbated following the recent conclusion of the bilateral agreement with the EU. The experience of economic unification in the EU suggests, however, that labour market mobility in Europe is relatively stable, particularly among unskilled workers.

This implies that there would be little risk that application of this agreement would lead to a large influx of workers from EU countries. Moreover, should the level of immigration be considered problematic, the agreement provides for the temporary reduction of quotas as a safeguard.

Overall, the experience of Switzerland suggests that globalization tends to aggravate the perverse effects of domestic policy distortions, such as the relatively weak product-market competition environment that has long prevailed in the country. Interestingly, the Government has undertaken reforms in this area that are broadly in parallel with the EU, with which it conducts the bulk of its trade. This provides a vivid illustration of how developments in the EU have a bearing on Swiss legislation and economic policy, even though the country does not participate in the EU's decision-making process.

BIBLIOGRAPHY

Addison, J.; Fox, D.; Ruhm, C. 1996. *Trade sensitivity, technology and labor displacement*, Working Paper No. 5621. Cambridge, Massachusetts, National Bureau of Economic Research (NBER).

Altman, R.C. 1998. "The nuke of the 90s", in *New York Times Magazine*, Mar.

Anker, R.; Paratian, R.; Torres, R. 2001. *Mauritius: Country studies on the social dimensions of globalization.* Geneva, ILO.

Bakkenist Management Consultants. 1998. *Temporary work businesses in the countries of the European Union.* Brussels, International Confederation of Temporary Work Businesses.

Bank for International Settlements. 1998. *Central Bank survey of foreign exchange and derivatives market activity in April 1998: Preliminary global data.* Basle.

Borensztein, B.; de Gregorio, J.; Lee, J.-W. 1995. *How does foreign direct investment affect economic growth?*, Working Paper No. 5057. Cambridge, Massachusetts, NBER.

Charnovitz, S. 1987. "The influence of international labour standards on the world trading regime: A historical overview", in *International Labour Review*, Vol. 126, No. 5, pp. 565–584.

Commonwealth Secretariat. 1998. *The trade implications for small vulnerable States of the global trade regime shift: Final report, Terms of reference.* London.

Currie, J.; Harrison, A. 1997. "Sharing the costs: The impact of trade reform on capital and labour in Morocco", in *Journal of Labor Economics*, Vol. 15, No. 3, Part II, Suppl., pp. 44–71.

De Long, B. 1998. *What's wrong with our bloody economies?* Jan.; mimeo.

Delsen, L. 1995. *Atypical employment: An international perspective. Causes, consequences and policy.* Groningen, Netherlands, Wolters-Noordhoff.

The Economist, 16 Jan. 1999.

Edwards, S. 1998. "Openness, productivity and growth: What do we really know?", in *Economic Journal*, Vol. 108, Mar., pp. 383–398.

European Commission. 1998. *European Economy*. Brussels, Directorate-General for Economic and Financial Affairs.

Eurostat. 1999. *Development of enterprises in Central European countries 1995–1997*. Luxembourg.

–. Various years. *Labour Force Survey*. Brussels.

Feenstra, R., Hanson, G. 1995. *Foreign investment, outsourcing and relative wages*, Working Paper No. 5121. Cambridge, Massachusetts, NBER.

Góra, M.; Rutkowski, M. 1998. *The quest for pension reform: Poland's security through diversity*, Warsaw, Office of the Government Plenipotentiary for Social Security Reform.

Hanson, G.; Harrison, A. 1995. *Trade, technology, and wage inequality*, Working Paper No. 5110. Cambridge, Massachusetts, NBER.

Hayter, S.; Reinecke, G.; Torres, R. 2001. *South Africa: Country studies on the social dimensions of globalization*. Geneva, ILO.

Humphrey, J. 1998. *Globalization and supply chain networks in the auto industry: Brazil and India*, Paper prepared for the International Workshop on "Global Production and Local Jobs". Geneva, International Institute for Labour Studies.

International Labour Office (ILO). 1996. *World Employment 1996/97: National policies in a global context*. Geneva.

–. 1998. Declaration on Fundamental Principles and Rights at Work and its Follow-up. Geneva.

–. Various years. *Panorama Laboral*. Lima.

–, Governing Body. Various years. Documents of the Working Party on the Social Dimensions of the Liberalization of Trade: GB.267/WP/SDL/1/1 (Nov. 1996); GB.268/WP/SDL/1/2 (Mar. 1997); GB.270/WP/SDL/1/2 (Nov. 1997); GB.273/WP/SDL/2 (Nov. 1998).

International Monetary Fund (IMF). 1998 (Oct.); 1999 (May). *World Economic Outlook*. Washington, DC.

–. 1999. *International Financial Statistics*, CD-ROM. Washington, DC, Feb.

Knight, M. 1998. *Developing countries and the globalization of financial markets*, Working Paper No. 105. Washington, DC, IMF.

Lateef, A. 1997. *Linking up with the global economy: A case study of the Bangalore software industry*, Discussion Paper No. 96. Geneva, International Institute for Labour Studies.

Maddison, A. 1995. *Monitoring the world economy 1820–1992*. Paris, OECD.

Mello, L. de. 1997. "Foreign direct investment in developing countries and growth: A selective survey", in *Journal of Development Studies*, Vol. 34, No. 1, pp. 1–34.

Organisation for Economic Co-operation and Development (OECD). 1996. *Trade, employment and labour standards: A study of core workers' rights and international trade*. Paris.

–. 1998. *Open markets matter: The benefits of trade and investment liberalization.* Paris.

–. Various years. *Employment Outlook.* Paris.

Palpacuer, F. 1998. *Competitiveness, organizational changes and employment: A review of current trends and perspectives.* Geneva, ILO Task Force; mimeo.

Paratian, R.; Torres, R. 2001. *Bangladesh.: Country studies on the social dimensions of globalization.* Geneva, ILO.

Reinecke, G.; Torres, R. 2001. *Chile: Country studies on the social dimensions of globalization.* Geneva, ILO.

Robbins, D. 1996. *Evidence on trade and wages in the developing world*, Technical Paper, No. 119. Paris, OECD.

Rodrik, D. 1997. *Has globalization gone too far?* Washington, DC, Institute for International Economics.

Romero, A. T.; Torres, R. 2001. *Switzerland: Country studies on the social dimensions of globalization.* Geneva, ILO.

Servais, J.-M. 1989. "The social clause in trade agreements: Wishful thinking or an instrument of social progress?", in *International Labour Review*, Vol. 128, No. 4, pp. 423–432.

Tanzi, V. 1995. *Taxation in an integrated world.* Washington, DC, IMF.

Tokman, V.; Martínez, D. 1999. *Flexibilización en el margen: La reforma del contrato de trabajo.* Lima, ILO Regional Office for Latin America and the Caribbean.

Torres, R. 2000. "Trade and labour standards: an economic perspective", in US Department of Labor: *The social dimensions of economic integration: United States and European Union seminar on the social dimension of economic integration.* Washington, DC.

–. 2001. *Republic of Korea: Country studies on the social dimensions of globalization.* Geneva, ILO.

–; et al. 2001. *Poland: Country studies on the social dimensions of globalization.* Geneva, ILO.

United Nations Conference on Trade and Development (UNCTAD). Various years. *World Investment Report.* New York and Geneva.

United Nations Industrial Development Organization (UNIDO). 1999. Industrial Statistics Database. Vienna.

Weller, J. 1998. *Los mercados laborales en América Latina: Su evolución en el largo plazo y sus tendencias recientes.* Santiago, Economic Commission for Latin America and the Caribbean (ECLAC).

Wood, A. 1997. "Openness and wage inequality in developing countries: The Latin American challenge to East Asian conventional wisdom", in *World Bank Economic Review*, Vol. 11, No. 1, pp. 33–57.

World Bank. 1998, 1999. *World Development Indicators*, CD-ROM. Washington, DC.

World Trade Organization (WTO). 1996. *Singapore Ministerial Declaration*, WTO Ministerial Conference, Singapore 9–13 Dec. WT/MIN(96)/DEC/W, 13 Dec. Geneva.

–. 1998. *Implementation of WTO provisions in favour of developing country members*, Note by the Secretariat, Committee on Trade and Development, WT/COMTD/W/35. Geneva.

INDEX

Note: Page numbers in **bold** refer to major text sections, those in *italic* to figures, tables and boxes. Subscript numbers appended to page numbers indicate an endnote, the letter *n* a footnote. Concatenated page numbers (eg 17–19) do not necessarily indicate continuous treatment.

Other books on the social dimensions of globalization

World Employment Report 2001: Life at work in the information economy

This important flagship study examines the employment challenges and opportunities emerging from the rapid growth of information and communication technologies (ICTs). Recognized as among the major drivers of economic growth and wealth creation, ICTs are raising productivity, reducing costs and increasing the speed of communications to help shape the new global economy. Their effects on the emergence of new enterprise and the demand for new skills and knowledge are profound, and this study illustrates how they are changing labour market conditions as well as industrial relations. However, the new technologies could potentially worsen national and global inequalities through an increasing "digital divide". The *Report* addresses these concerns and identifies important strategies and policy measures that can be taken to ensure that ICTs lead to development, poverty alleviation and decent work.

The *World Employment Report 2001* is the fourth in a series of ILO reports which offer an international perspective on current employment issues.

Publication June 2001
Available in book and CD-ROM form
ISBN 92-2-111630-1

350 pp., softcover

Other books on the social dimensions of globalization

World Labour Report 1999–2000: Income security in a changing world

The *World Labour Report 1999–2000* examines the changing context in which women and men are trying to achieve income security for themselves and their families. Drawing on detailed, worldwide data, the report assesses the impact of globalization and liberalization, and considers the vital role played by social protection in supporting, supplementing and replacing market incomes. In the process, it re-evaluates the relationship between social protection and the economy, and addresses the challenge of finding the most effective means to bring social protection to the majority who still go without.

ISBN 92-2-110831-7

2000   330 pp.   softcover

Other books on the social dimensions of globalization

World Employment Report 1998–99 Employability in the global economy : How training matters

The *World Employment Report 1998–99* reviews the global employment situation and examines how countries in different circumstances and stages of development can develop the best training strategy and flexible and responsive training systems to address these far-reaching changes. The report presents a close analysis of training systems world-wide and an examination of training strategies for increasing national competitiveness, improving the efficiency of enterprises and promoting employment growth. It critically examines policies and targeted pro-grammes for improving women's employment opportunities and enhancing the skills and employability of informal sector workers and members of vulnerable groups (especially at-risk youth, long-term unemployed, older displaced workers and workers with disabilities). The report suggests specific policy reforms for making training more efficient and effective. Given the rapid and continuous pace of change in the demand for new skills, the report concludes that training and lifelong learning need to be given higher priority. The best results from enhancing the education and skill levels of the workforce are achieved in an overall growth-promoting environment and when trainng decisions are taken in close consultations between government, employers and workers.

The *World Employment Report 1998–99* is the third in a series of ILO reports which offer an international perspective on current employment issues.

ISBN 92-2-110827-9

1998   271 pp., softcover

Other books on the social dimensions of globalization

Key Indicators of the Labour Market (KILM)

This valuable, wide-ranging reference tool meets the ever-increasing demand for timely, accurate and accessible information on the rapidly changing world of work. *Key Indicators of the Labour Market* (KILM) provides the general reader, as well as the expert, with concise explanations and analysis of the data on the world`s labour markets.

Harvesting vast information from international data repositories and regional and national statistical sources, KILM offers data on a broad range of countries for the years 1980 and 1990, and all available subsequent years. Using statistical data on the labour force, employment, unemployment, underemployment, educational attainment of the workforce, wages and compensation, productivity and labour costs, and poverty and income distribution as market indicators, it also includes overviews of topics such as employment-to-population ratios, hours of work, youth unemployment, wages in manufacturing, labour productivity and costs, and gender issues. By highlighting multiple labour market indicators, this comprehensive resource sheds light on equity and other job concerns as well.

KILM is available in three formats – standard print version, CD-ROM, and (in 2001) Web. The interactive design of the CD-ROM and Web versions allows users to customize their searches by any combination of indicator, country, year, or data inputs.

1999 edition: ISBN 92-2-110834-1 CD-ROM
           92-2-110833-1 book (600 pp., softcover)
2001 edition to be published in September 2001